ISBN- 9798797084792

First Printing - January 6, 2022
Second Printing - March 12, 2022
Third Printing - May 15, 2022
Fourth Printing - Dec 1, 2022

Printed in the United States of America

INTRODUCTION

*"A new **poll** from The Washington Post and the University of Maryland found 51 percent of Americans think the legal repercussions for those who forced their way into the U.S. Capitol last year have "not been harsh enough." Fewer than 2 in 10 Americans told surveyors that the punishments are "too harsh" while 28 percent said they believed the consequences to be fair."*

I'm a late-stage Baby Boomer and I grew up thinking of the Federal government as the folks who wore the white hats. We won the war, built an inter-state highway system second to none, and in areas like school segregation, integration, and voting rights, the Federal government led the nation in a moral re-thinking of how we treated others. It was an honor to be an American.

Somewhere along the way, things changed. Maybe it was Vietnam when we learned that the Federal government was "cooking the books" with false claims of casualties, or maybe Watergate, which was really the actions of a few people but somehow it tainted the government itself, or maybe the Oliver North revelations that the government was working with drug lords, or maybe J. Edgar's penchant to use the FBI to illegally spy on people he disliked. In any event, my perceptions of the Federal government changed. Not that the feds had become the mustachio villains on black horses, but clearly the Federal government was no longer, by definition, the good guy.

Four years with Donald Trump didn't help improve the image of the Federal government but even the shock and awe of those years didn't prepare me for what I would find when I obsessively delved into what happened on January 6, 2021. My initial interest was in the characteristics of the people who participated in the event. As a Clinical Psychologist and a researcher, I was compelled to look at who these people were and what their motivations were, and the results of that journey were summarized in three books – two on the rioters and one on the riot. In the summer of 2021, as defendants began to accept plea agreements and as the trickle of sentences began to spin circles in the judicial pond, I got interested in what was happening within the Justice system. The more I looked, the more the data insisted I looked more intensely. This book is the result.

If you believe what happened on Jan 6 wasn't a riot and that many of the people arrested that date were not intent on obstructing the lawful progress of constitutionally derived processes, then this is a suitable time to stop reading.

It can be argued that it's too early to draw conclusions. After all, nearly two years after the fact, slightly more than 900 of the estimated 3,000 people have been arrested, and of those 900+ only about half pleaded guilty to charges and only slightly more than 300 were sentenced. Overtime, these numbers will increase, and future research will probably uncover additional findings. But at this point there is enough data, and the trends are so convincing that publication at this time makes sense.

Many people have expressed concern that the sentences being given out to the Jan 6 rioters are too lenient, and these concerns come not only from everyday people but from elected officials, lawyers, prosecutors, and even Judges. Not only the sentences themselves have come under question, but nearly two years after the event, fewer than one third of the estimated rioters have even been identified and only slightly more than 900 have been arrested and 300+ sentenced. Of those sentenced, about half got any jail time at all, and the median jail sentence was only 45 days. Is this the proper response to an event in which hundreds of armed and angry people, forecasting their intentions to commit violence, invaded the Capitol, assaulted, and injured hundreds of Police and caused multiple millions of dollars of damage, in an attempt to disrupt the lawful process of American electoral law?

Let's begin with a discussion of what exactly happened, and then try to describe the behavior in legal terms. Having achieved an understanding of what happened and what the appropriate charges should be, we'll examine the decisions by the Department of Justice (DOJ) and the critical steps in the legal process, and then look at the behavior of the Attorney General and the Judges. Along the way we'll describe who these people were, examining their personal characteristics, motivations, and behavior.

This is a perilous journey, so you need to be prepared. America is at an unprecedented critical time when the very principles upon which this Nation was founded are being tested. We must meet this test head-on, and we need our Justice system to rise to the occasion. Failure to properly deal with the events of January 6 will be a grim foreboding for the future of the Nation. Indeed, for the future of the world.

WHAT HAPPENED?

"Trump's motives are clear enough. We don't need a degree in advanced psychiatry to know that a sociopathic megalomaniac must always win; nothing else can be contemplated." **Noam Chomsky**

Legal scholars debate whether the behavior of the people who invaded the Capitol amounts to "treason" or "sedition" or "seditious conspiracy" or what. This debate is important because based on the definition of what took place, from that the appropriate responses can be determined.

Republican Senator Ron Johnson (WI) said January 6 was "not an armed insurrection and it was, by-and-large, peaceful." Republican Representative Andrew Clyde (GA) compared parts of the riot to a "normal tourist visit" saying that TV footage of the insurrection "showed people in an orderly fashion staying between the stanchions and ropes taking videos and pictures." If January 6, 2021, was simply a "MAGA tourist" event, as these Republican lawmakers suggest, the idea of sentencing people to jail time seems disproportionate and even ludicrous. If, on the other hand, their actions constituted "treason," as Judge Chutkan argued when sentencing one of the defendants, then a median of 45 days in jail seems like a slap in the face to the American people.

To understand what happened and to put it into a proper perspective from which to judge whether the January 6 event was a planned violent attempt to interrupt the democratic process or simply a rally gone bad, we need to look at the antecedents.

The major reason expressed by people arrested who came to D.C. on Jan 6 was to protest the election which they considered fraudulent. My data indicates that more than 30% of the people arrested claimed protesting the election was the reason for attending. No other reason (e.g., supporting Trump, protesting government, filming the event, looking to harm Antifa) was as pervasive. Hence, if the election was the prime cause for people coming to D.C. on January 6, it will help understanding what happened by reviewing the circumstances surrounding the election.

ANTICIPATING LOSS

Even before the election occurred, Trump began saying that the only way he would lose was if there was fraud. Here's a timeline –

- April 7, 2020. Trump said – ***"Mail ballots are a very dangerous thing for this country, because they're cheaters..."*** Trump neglected to say that he votes by mail.
- June 25, 2020. Attorney General Barr questions the possibilities of counterfeit mail-in ballots, but admits he has no evidence.
- July 19, 2020. Trump said - ***"...mail-in voting is going to rig the election."*** When asked if he would accept the results he said - ***"I'm not going to just say yes. I'm not going to say no."***
- July 2020 – Brad Parscale (Trump Campaign Manager) to J6C – ***"Trump planned as early as July that he would say he won the election even if he lost."***
- Aug 17, 2020. Trump said - ***"The only way we're going to lose this election is if the election is rigged"***
- Sept. 10, 2020. In an interview with Alex Jones on his InfoWars program, Trump confidant Roger Stone called for martial law if Trump were to lose the election.
- Sept. 12, 2020. In an interview at the White House with Fox News' Jeanine Pirro, Trump was asked what he would do in the event Americans "threaten riots" in

response to his winning the election. He replied: *"We'll put them down very quickly if they do that…. We have the right to do that, we have the power to do that if we want. Look, it's called insurrection."*

- Sept. 23, 2020. In response to a direct question, Trump refuses to say he would ensure a peaceful transfer of power if he lost the election.
- Oct 22, 2020. Secretary of Defense Esper worries that his talks with Trump indicate Trump might use the National Guard if he lost the election, so he alerts all 50 State National Guard heads to notify him if they were "directed to do something out of the normal."
- Oct 31, 2020. Tom Fitton e-mail draft statement to Molly Michael and Dan Scavino for Trump to issue after election – *"I won [based on] the ballots counted by the Election Day deadline."* There is no "election day deadline" but Trump advisers anticipated that as more ballots were counted Trump would lose due to mail-in votes usually going to Democrats.
- Oct 31, 2020. Steve Bannon recorded on video – *"Trump is gonna do is declare victory…That doesn't mean he won…He's gong to sit right there and say they stole it…Trump is going to do some crazy shit."*
- Nov 1, 2020. Trump key-adviser Roger Stone says - *"It will still be up in the air. The key thing is to declare victory. We won. Fuck you"*

THE POST-ELECTION CLAIMS

- Nov 3, 2020. Trump said *"…we did win this election… we want all voting to stop."* At that point it was "up for grabs," but mail-in votes were turning the tide in Biden's favor.
- Nov 3. 2020. Trump adviser Steve Bannon wrote - *"You know why they're going to steal this election? Because*

they don't think you're going to do anything about it."

- Nov 14-15, 2020. According to testimony from Oath Keepers leader Joshua James, he met with Stuart Rhodes to begin plans to *"forcefully block the transfer of power."*
- Nov 15, 2020. Trump tweeted from the golf course - *"... the Election was Rigged... [Biden] only won in the eyes of the FAKE NEWS MEDIA...I concede NOTHING!"*
- Nov 19, 2020. Trump's lawyer Rudy Giuliani speaking about the election said - *"I know crimes. I can smell them. You don't have to smell this one. I can prove it to you 18 different ways."* (He never did it 1 way, much less 18).
- Nov 19, 2020. Trump calls Georgia's Secretary of State and pleads for Raffensberger to find him 11,780 votes.
- Nov 29, 2020. Trump tweeted - *"NO WAY WE LOST THIS ELECTION!*
- Dec 1, 2020. A full-page ad in the Washington Times urged Trump to *"immediately declare a limited form of Martial Law, and temporarily suspend the Constitution and civilian control of these federal elections, for the sole purpose of having the military oversee a re-vote."*
- Dec 7, 2020. "Alternative elector" slates for Arizona appear at the National Archives. Along with alternative slates for a half dozen other states, they are rejected as forgeries.
- Dec 8, 2020. VP Pence's lawyer Gregory Jacob responds to a request from the VP about his role in the Electoral College vote, anticipating the pressure Trump and others will place upon him on Jan 6. On Jan 5 Jacobs will once address the issue and warn Pence that following Eastman's advice would be illegal.
- Dec 12, 2020. At a "Stop the Steal" rally, Oath Keeper founder Stewart Rhodes calls on Trump to invoke the Insurrection Act. He posts - *"Either Trump gets off his ass and uses the insurrection Act to defeat the ChiCom puppet coup or we will have to rise up in insurrection*

> *(rebllion) against the ChiCom puppet Biden. Take your pick."*

- Dec 18, 2020. Trump meets in the White House to discuss possibilities of invoking the Insurrection Act, suggested by retired General Mike Flynn.
- Dec 20, 2020. Flynn and lawyer Sidney Powell participate in WH meeting discussing seizing voting machines. The idea is rejected after WH Counsel Pat Cipollone points out that the act was illegal.
- Dec 22, 2020. Texas Rep. Louis Gohmert filed a lawsuit seeking a judicial judgment that VP Pence had constitutional power to handle competing slates. The lawsuit was dismissed.
- Dec 28, 2020. Roger Stone posts on Parler – *"I also told the President exactly how he can…to ensure Donald Trump continues as our President."*

EVIDENCE FROM THE COURTS

The best sole source for information about the lawsuits trying to establish that the election was "stolen" is on Wikipedia. Here's their summary –

"Nearly all the suits were dismissed or dropped due to lack of evidence; judges, lawyers, and other observers described the suits as "frivolous" and "without merit". In one instance, the Trump campaign and other groups seeking his reelection collectively lost multiple cases in six states on a single day. Only one ruling was initially in Trump's favor: the timing within which first-time Pennsylvania voters must provide proper identification if they wanted to "cure" their ballots. This ruling affected very few votes, and it was later overturned by the Pennsylvania Supreme Court."

Here are a few highlights of the court actions -

- Nov 13, 2020. MI Chief Justice Timothy Kenny rejected

Trump's claims and said - *"'Plaintiffs' interpretation of events is incorrect and not credible."*

- Nov 21, 2020. PA Federal Judge Matthew Brann rejected Trump lawsuit. He said - *"This claim, like Frankenstein's Monster, has been haphazardly stitched together . . . This Court has been presented with strained legal arguments without merit and speculative accusations, unpled in the operative complaint and unsupported by evidence."*
- Nov 27, 2020. Trump-appointed PA judge Stephanos Bibas rejected Trump lawsuit and said - *"Charges of unfairness are serious. But calling an election unfair does not make it so. Charges require specific allegations and then proof. We have neither here."*

EVIDENCE FROM GOVERNMENT AGENCIES

- Nov 9, 2020. Trump's Attorney General (AG) William Barr sent a memo that federal prosecutors should investigate election fraud cases. 16 US Attorneys responded by saying they found no substantial problems.
- Nov 12, 2020. The Dept. Homeland Security Cybersecurity Head Chris Krebs said - *"The November 3rd election was the most secure in American history... There is no evidence that any voting system deleted or lost votes, changed votes, or was in any way compromised."* Trump fired him a week later.
- Nov 12, 2020. Benjamin Hovland, Commissioner of Election Commission said - *"We never see evidence of widespread voter fraud. And there's no indicators that 2020 will be different in that regard."*
- Nov 23, 2020. GSA Head Emily Murphy sent Biden a letter - *"...the transition can begin."*
- Dec 1, 2020. Trump's AG William Barr said - *"To date,*

[DOJ investigators] have not seen fraud on a scale that could have effected a different outcome in the election."

- Jan 5, 2021. Mark Meadows, WH Chief of Staff, shared a 36-page PowerPoint report - "Election Fraud, Foreign Interference & Options for 6 Jan" –among top White House officials and Republican lawmakers. The paper urged a "national security emergency" be declared.

TRUMP KNEW THE TRUTH

Despite all the talk and all the lawsuits, there is considerable evidence that Trump knew all along that he lost -

- Nov 10, 2020. Alyssa Farah (WH Communications Director) to J6C – *"A week after the election…he looked at the TV and said 'Can you believe I lost to that fucking guy'?"*
- Cassidy Hutchinson to J6C – Mark Meadows said *"he [Trump] pretty much acknowledges that he lost."*
- Nov 20, 2020. Alex Cannon (Trump Campaign Manager) to J6C about a conversation with Mark Meadows – *"We weren't finding anything that could be sufficient to change the results in any of the key states."*
- Dec 31, 2020. Memo from Trump attorney John Eastman – *"…the President signed a verification…on Dec 1, he has since been made aware that some of the allegations (and evidence proffered by the experts) has been inaccurate…"*
- Dec 24, 2020. Cassidy Hutchinson to J6C – *"…and the President said, I don't want people to know that we lost."*
- Dec 24, 2020. General Milley (Joint Chiefs) to J6C recounting meeting with Trump – *"Yeah, we lost."*
- Dec 31, 2020. Trump attorney Kenneth Chesebro in an e-mail to Trump legal team - *"We want to frame things so that [Clarence] Thomas could be the one to issue*

some sort of stay or other circuit justice opinion saying Georgia is in legitimate doubt...our only chance to get a favorable judicial opinion by Jan. 6, which might hold up the Georgia count in Congress."

CHAPTER SUMMARY

Anticipating loss, six months before the election Trump began laying the foundation for his claim that the election would be fraudulent.

As results came in, Trump declared victory despite the numbers and he continues to this day to claim he won.

Eventually he lost by 7,052,771 votes (81,268,925 vs. 74,216,154) or 9.5%. In 2016 he lost by 2,864,903 votes or 4.35% but he won the electoral votes 304 vs. 227. In 2020 he lost the electoral votes by 306 vs. 232.

Trump's 9.5% loss in the popular vote was the second largest loss in the six Presidential elections in the 21 st Century.

Trump and his supporters initiated more than 60 lawsuits but failed to win a single case, often withdrawing the case and when heard, often dismissed with harsh comments from the Judges.

Trump and his supporters attempted to influence the state agencies responsible for appointing Electoral College representatives, but failed.

Trump and his supporters helped initiate reviews and re-assessments of election results in several states, with no discernable changes in results and no proof of more than the usual malpractice.

The DOJ and the Cybersecurity Branch of the federal government initiated investigations and found no evidence of unusual practices and nothing that would change any results.

Short of a military coup, the only remaining obstacle to Biden being appointed President was the January 6 joint meeting of both houses of Congress to certify the results. If a rally-turned-riot could cause the Politicians to violate the law, Trump could remain in power. If the violence got out of control, Trump could declare martial law and remain in power. It seemed like a win-win situation for a President obsessed with staying in power.

INTENTIONS TO VIOLENCE

"Some perpetrators tackled and dragged law enforcement officers. Among the many examples of such violence: One officer was crushed in a door. Another was dragged down a set of stairs, face down, repeatedly tased and beaten, and suffered a heart attack. Some perpetrators attacked law enforcement officers with chemical agents that burned their eyes and skin, and some assaulted officers with pipes, poles, and other dangerous or deadly weapons." **AG Garland, Jan 6, 2022**

One of the critical steps to take in discussing the Jan 6 riot is whether it was a planned riot or whether a peaceful and legitimate political rally went sideways. To assess whether the participants planned on or expected the event to result in violence, I examined the FBI and DOJ records and news media reports on the event, looking at three factors: (1) participants wearing combat gear or using combat equipment, (2) participants wearing disguises, and (3) pre-riot social media reports indicating that the participants expected violence.

In looking at the data, I separated the participants into three groups – violent offenders, non-violent men, and women. As of November 2022, the violent offender group had over 200 people, 9 of whom were women. The non-violent group had over 500 men and the women's group had 135 women (2 of whom were dead at the scene).

Inter-rater reliability on all 3 measures exceeded 90%. Here are the results-

COMBAT GEAR

Combat gear was easy to identify – tactical vests, body armor, helmets (some with face shields), combat boots, weapons (e.g., tasers, sprays, guns, rifles, explosives), communications gear, etc. In some cases, it was necessary to get the information from FBI reports because the gear was not readily seen in the photos.

DISGUISES

Disguises also were easy to identify, though no one who simply wore a Covid-19 mask was included in this category, and people who wore costumes that showed their faces also were not included.

SOCIAL MEDIA

Pre-riot social media comments were difficult to obtain since almost all the posts were deleted by the participants; however, FBI documents did include pre-riot social media comments for about one fourth of the participants. Almost every pre-riot social media comment covered by the FBI contained references to the expectation of violence.

Here are the social media posts by rioters prior to the Jan 6 meeting. Most people had multiple posts. For purposes of space, this list contains only one illustrative post per person rather than all the posts. The data is presented chronologically without corrections for spelling and grammar. **People in bold** were originally charged with violent behavior.

Oct 14, 2020. Book store clerk Rachel Powell (40, Sandy Lake, PA) posts on FB – "I agree with the possibility of civil war happening. I can see that too. Unfortunately, the only way this is probably capable of being fixed is bloodshed because I'm not so sure our government can be fixed the political way anymore either." She later posts a photo carrying a gun.

Oct 30, 2020. Proud Boys sympathizer 49-year-old Lisa A Homer (Scottsdale, AZ) wrote on Instagram - "Letsblowshipup." (sic). She will show up on Jan 6 wearing a camouflage helmet, goggles, and a tactical vest. She'll plead guilty to "Parading."

Nov 2020, Phillip Bromley (46, Sterrett, AL) texted - "...the punishment for treason is death...be ready for the physical fight to come." In December he'll post – "Let's kill all the commie bastards..." He'll plead guilty to "Disorderly" and sentenced to 90 days jail, $3,500 fine, and 12 months' probation.

Nov 2, 2020. Michael Daugherty (58, Pelham, GA) who owned "Crazy Coon's Armory" posted - "Anyone needing an AR15 and some extra ammo before the election, I've got a couple left in stock. ... It may be your last chance if the election don't (sic) go right tomorrow!" He'll plead guilty to "Entering," sentenced to 3 years' probation, 60 hours community service, and 60 days house arrest.

Nov 2, 2020. On election day **Jordan Mink** (27, Oakdale PA) posted a photo with a gun and noted – "The ballot is stronger than the bullet...my magazines will be fully loaded just in case it's not." On Jan 6 he'll use a baseball bat to shatter windows.

Nov 3, 2020. The day after the election **Christopher Quaglin** (35, North Brunswick NJ) wrote on FB - "I'm going to war...I'm writing my letter to my wife and people will have it. But I might not even make it back." The next day he wrote – "Looking forward to a war." On Jan 6 he will attack Police with pepper spray. Weeks later Police will find a gun room which Quaglin claims he started after Obama was elected.

Nov 3, 2020. **Christian Secor** (22, Costa Mesa, CA) - "We're gonna win bigly and if we don't we're taking this ship down in flames." More than a year later he'll plead guilty to "obstruction."

Nov 4, 2020. **Marshall Neefe** (25, Newville, PA) wrote to

Charles Smith – "I'm getting ready to storm D.C." On Jan 6 he showed up with a wooden club. He'll plead guilty to "Assault with a Deadly Weapon," and get 41 months' jail and 3 years' probation.

Nov 4, 2020. Troy Smocks (58, Dallas, TX), one of the few Black people arrested, wrote on Parler - "[I]t's time to physically bite them, while there is still enough of us to form a strong resistance." He'll plead guilty to "Assault with a Deadly Weapon," and get 41 months' jail and 3 years' probation.

Nov 5, 2020. **Joseph Biggs** (38, Ormond Beach, FL) posted – "It's time for fucking War…"

Nov 5, 2020. Oath Keeper leader Elmer Stuart Rhodes (56, Granbury, TX) sent an encrypted message on Signal - "We aren't getting through this without a civil war. Too late for that." On Dec 11 he added – "…it will be a bloody and desperate fight. We are going to have a fight. That can't be avoided." Rhodes was charged with "seditious conspiracy" in Jan 2022 along with 10 other Oath Keepers.

Nov 5, 2020. Matthew Bledsoe (38, Memphis, TN), owner of a moving company, posted – "Trump won, riots will start again soon…" A jury will find him guilty of Obstruction and three more charges.

Nov 6, 2020. Andrew Hernandez (44, Riverside, CA), one of the few non-Whites arrested, posted – "If people do not fight now go out and protest the vote/election fraud. [sic] Than your voting days are over." He'll plead guilty to "Obstruction" and is awaiting sentencing.

Nov 7, 2020. Former Policeman Thomas Robertson (47, Ferrum, VA) wrote – "…a legitimate republic stands on 4 boxes. The soapbox, the ballot box, the jury box, and then the cartridge box…Im (sic) about to become part of one…" A jury will find him guilty of "Obstruction", "Civil Disorder" and 3 more charges and sentence him to 8 years' jail.

Nov 12, 2020. Attorney William Calhoun (57, Americus, GA) wrote – "…it's going to be hard to buy a beer when Democrats are being shot on site [sic]…we are going to kill every last communist who stands in Trump's way." Following his arrest, the FBI found an arsenal of weapons.

Nov 17, 2020. Ohio Oath Keeper Jessica Watkins (38, Woodstock, OH) said - "… it is our duty as Americans to fight, kill and die for our rights." She added "I need you fighting fit by innaugeration (sic)." She was charged with "seditious conspiracy" in Jan 2022 along with 10 other Oath Keepers and elected a Jury trial.

Nov 25, 2020. **Enrique Tarrio** (38, Miami, FL) posted – "…the American people are at war with YOU [Biden]…No peace. No Quarter."

Nov 23, 2020. Karl Dresch (40, Calumet, MI), a convicted felon, wrote on FB - "It's war everywhere if we let this election get stolen." FBI search of his home found weapons and ammunition. He'll plead guilty to "Parading" and sentenced to 6 months' jail.

Nov 25, 2020. **Kelly O'Brien**, (49, North Whitehall, PA) one of the few females arrested for violent behavior, wrote – "The O'Brien armory is well stocked. Just in case. These idiot's [sic] don't even realize how hard it is to buy bullets. They're gone. We ain't worried." She'll plead guilty to "Entering," sentenced to 3 months' jail, 12 months' probation and $1,000 fine.

Nov 27, 2000. Proud Boy **Zach Rehl** (35, Philadelphia) on Parler – "Hopefully the firing squads are for the traitors that are trying to steal the election…" He'll be charged with "Obstruction", "Conspiracy" and "Destruction."

Dec 2020. Robert Reeder (55, Rockville, MD) wrote - "Civil war is coming. This time the conservatives will stand their ground and the radicals will die." He'll plead guilty to "Parading", sentenced to

3 months' jail.

Dec 2020. **Joshua James** (33, Arab, Alabama) posted a photo of guns and ammunition on Parler. Robert Minuta (36, NY tattoo artist) replied - "I've been hoarding any ammo I can get my hands on lol." On Jan 6 they met up. Both were arrested. He pleaded guilty to seditious conspiracy. He'll plead guilty to "Seditious Conspiracy" and "Obstruction" – awaiting sentencing.

Dec 4, 2020. Russel Peterson (34, Rochester, PA) on FB – "The only way to restore balance and peace is through war. Too much Trust has been lost in our great nation." He'll plead guilty to "Parading", sentenced to 30 days' jail.

Dec 5, 2020. Oath Keeper Brian Ulrich (43, Guyton, GA) messaged - "I seriously wonder what it would take just to get ever patriot marching around the capital armed! Just to show our government how powerless they are!" A few days later he posts – "I'll be the guy running around with the budget AR." He'll plead guilty to "Seditious Conspiracy" and "Obstruction" – awaiting sentencing.

Dec. 10, 2020. Damon Beckley (Louisville, KY) registered a limited liability company called D.C. Under Siege with the Kentucky Secretary of State.

Dec 12, 2020. Anti-vaxxer and former Police Chief Alan Hostetter (56, San Clemente, CA) speaking at a "Stop the Steal" rally said - "The enemies and traitors of America, both foreign and domestic, must be held accountable, and they will. There must be long prison terms, while execution is the just punishment for the ringleaders of this coup." On Jan 6 Hostetter will coordinate movements for the 3%ers.

Dec 12, 2020. Unemployed fitness clerk Thomas Baranyi (29, Ewing, NJ) texts - "They [politicians] have to be removed. By force. That's the only way." Later he adds - "Bludgeon thru them to get to the Government that's the only way left." He'll plead guilty to

"Entering", sentenced to 3 months' jail, 12 months' probation, and 60 hours community service.

Dec 14, 2020. Brittiany Dillon (35, Oklahoma City, OK) texts - "We may lose all communications. An all out civil war may start. It will be fast because our side is more prepared." She'll plead guilty to "Disorderly", sentenced to 3 years' probation and 60 days house arrest.

Dec 14, 2020. **William Wilson** (45, Newton Grove, NC) wrote on Signal – "It is time to fight." On Jan 5, 2021 he added "That's why I have all my gear with me." He'll plead guilty to "Seditious Conspiracy" and "Obstruction" – awaiting sentencing.

Dec 16, 2020. Corrine Montoni (31, Lakeland, FL) posted on FB that "they" were "getting close" and when asked "Close to what?" she replied, "To what…The Revolution."

Dec 19, 2020. Federal firearms dealer Matthew Loganbill (55, Versailles, MO) on FB - "They haven't seen a riot, til our side gets started." On Jan 6 he showed up with a gas mask and combat helmet. He'll plead guilty to "Obstruction" - awaiting sentencing.

Dec 20, 2020. 30-year-old Rachel Myers ((30, PA) wrote on FB – "I am totally fine with Civil War…It's beyond time"

Dec 20, 2020. **Tim Boughner** (41, MI) posted on Target – "…we are going to be at war." He'll be charged with using pepper spray on officers.

Dec 21, 2021. Jacob Garcia (27, Burleson, TX) - "Get ready DC…IT'S TIME TO RISE THE F***UP."

Dec 22, 2021. Proud Boy **Joshua Pruitt** (39, Washington D.C.) chatted - "I'm ready to fk shit up lol." Shortly after, he was arrested and charged with threatening his girlfriend. Undeterred, on Dec 31 he wrote - "bought a damn mma mouth guard, got my wrist Straps and a glove so I don't break my fking hands on one of these pussies."

Dec. 24, 2020. Retired Air Force Lt. Col. Larry Brock (53, Fort Worth, TX) posted on FB - "Bought body armor for the civil war that's coming." On Jan 1 he posted – "Castle will be stormed on the 6 th ."

Dec 24, 2020. The day before Christmas, Marine veteran **Ryan Nichols** (30, Longview, TX) posted on FB – "By Bullet or Ballot, Restoration of the Republic is Coming." On Jan 6 he used a spray aerosol against Police. His co-conspirator, Alex Harkrider (33, Carthage TN) posted they were "planning a civil war."

Dec 26, 2020. Stephen Ayres posted on FB - "If the [DS] robs president Trump!!! Civil War will ensue!" He'll plead guilty to "Disorderly," sentenced to 2 years' probation. He also testified at the Jan 6 Commission, blaming Trump for his actions.

Dec 26, 2020. Athanasios Zoyganeles posted – "hell not the game not over. The people are storming Washington D.C on the 6." On Jan 5, 2021. He added - "We need to take over the capital [sic] building tomorrow." He'll plead guilty to "Parading" – awaiting sentencing.

Dec 27, 2020. **Ethan Nordean** (30, Auburn, WA) using his alias "Rufio Panman" posted on Parler – "...things have gotten more dangerous for us this past year..." On Jan 4 he posted – "Let them remember the day they decided to make war with us." He added - "And fight we will...We are in a war."

Dec 28, 2020. Pamela Hemphill (68, Boise, ID) wrote on FB – "It's not going to be a FUN Trump Rally that is planned for January 6, it [sic] a WAR!" She'll plead guilty to "Parading," sentenced to 2 months' jail, 3 years' probation.

Dec 28, 2020. Rasha Abual-Ragbeh (40, Fairfield, NJ) who was born in Jordan and didn't even vote in 2020 posted – "Yeah bring your own guns if you will stay there by yourself there's no one with you from us, do you think BLM coming with no weapons? I'm bringing with me some toys also." She'll plead guilty to "Parading," sentenced to 3 years' probation, 60 hours community service, and 60 days house arrest.

Dec 29, 2020. Group message among Oat Keeper leadership - ***"They wont [sic] fear us until we come with rifles in hand."***

Dec 29, 2020. Edward Badalian (26, Los Angeles, CA) wrote on the Patriots 45 Group - "Congress can hang. I'll do it."

Dec 29, 2020. **Daniel Rodriguez** (38, Los Angeles, CA), one of the few Hispanics charged with violence, posted on Telegram - "Please let us get these people dear God."

Dec 29, 2020. **George Tenney** (35, Anderson, SC) wrote - "It's starting to look like we may siege the capital building and congress if the electoral votes don't go right..." He'll plead guilty to "Civil Disorder" and "Obstruction" - awaiting sentencing.

Dec 29, 2020. Robert Schornak (39, Roseville, MI) asked to borrow a bullet proof vest and wrote - "I'm going to DC on the 6 th and I don't expect it to be peaceful.They want a fight. Let's have it"

Dec 29, 2020. Jeremy Caplinger (25, Taylor, MI) posted - "I say storm the capitals(sic)." He'll plead guilty to "Climbing on U.S. Grounds" - sentenced to 35 days' jail, 2 years' probation, and 60 hours community service.

Dec 29, 2020. Glenn Croy (45, Colorado Springs, CO) texted – "me and dia are going to DC on the 6 to fight commies." He refers to his girlfriend as "dia". Both are arrested and both plead. He'll plead guilty to "Parading," sentenced to 14 days' jail, 3 years' probation, and 90 days house arrest.

Dec 29, 2020. Landon Mitchell (33, Houston, TX), one of the few Blacks arrested, posted - "If we don't fight now there is no point in ever voting again."

Dec 30, 2020. Lawrence Stackhouse (33, Blackwood, NJ) texted to Rachel Myers – "I'll give u a knife." He'll plead guilty to "Parading," sentenced to 14 days' jail, 3 years' probation and 90 days' house arrest.

Dec 30, 2020. Thomas Caldwell (65, Berryville, VA) wrote to Jessica Watkins – "…he is committed to being the quick reaction force and [sic] bringing the tools if something goes to hell. That way the boys don't have to schlep weps [sic] on the bus." Afterwards the FBI found Caldwell's hand-written "death list." He was charged with "seditious conspiracy" in Jan 2022 along with 10 other Oath Keepers and elected a Jury trial.

Dec 31, 2020. Luke Bender (21, Fairfax Station, VA) wrote on TikTok - "Patriots Its [sic] time to come together in D.C. And fight for our country. Just like our President Donald Trump has done for us. It's time we fight for him."

Dec 31, 2021. **Charles Bradford Smith** (25, Shippensburg, PA) messaged Marshall Neefe -"If it's big enough we should all just storm the buildings … Seriously." Later he said he was nailing a flag to an ax handle "so we can wave the flag but also have a giant beating stick just in case." He'll plead guilty to "Assault" and "Conspiracy" - sentenced to 41 months' jail and 3 years' probation.

Dec 31, 2020. Oath Keeper Edwards Vallejo (63, Phoenix, AZ) wrote to Oath Keeper leader Rhodes - "everyone has their own technical equipment and knows how to use it," adding a "winky face" emoji. Later he adds - "rifles" and "man power." Vallejo was charged with "seditious conspiracy" in Jan 2022.

Dec 31, 2021. West Virginia legislator Derrick Evans (35, Pritchard, WV) posts - "A STORM IS COMING…AND THERE IS NOTHING THE LEFT CAN DO TO STOP IT!" He'll plead guilty to "Obstruction during Civil Disorder" - sentenced to 3 months' jail, 3 years' probation and $2,000 fine.

Dec 31, 2020. **Nathaniel DeGrave** (32, Las Vegas) on FB – "Who can shoot and has excellent aim and can teach me today or tomorrow." He came to D.C. in combat gear, bear spray, and communications equipment. He pleaded guilty to assault and conspiracy.

Jan 1, 2020. **Justin Adams** (48, West Jordan, UT) on his way to D.C. posted - "smack a couple of politicians around..." Arrested in October 2022 and charged with Assault and Civil Disorder.

Jan 1, 2021. James Mels (56, Shelby Township, MI) texted why he was going to D.C. – "Hangings, Execution? Gitmo? We the people are getting our country back from these treasonous rat bastards ..." He'll plead guilty to "Entering" - awaiting sentencing.

Jan 1, 2021. Steven Thurlow, (50, St. Clair Shores, MI) wearing military gear, a firearm, and a "Boogaloo" patch, posts - "Ahh nothing like a new pair of 511's and fresh set of level IV SAPI's3 in the plate carrier to go 'peacefully protest' with."

Jan 2, 2021. **James Mault** (29, Fayetteville, NY), who was still in the Army at the time, told friends to arm themselves with batons, pepper spray, and "asskicking boots." On January 3, 2021, he told his codefendant, Cody Mattice, that he bought "pepper spray and a baton." Mault and Mattice will plead guilty to "Assault" - sentenced to 44 months' jail and 3 years' probation.

Jan 2, 2021. Mark Grods (54, Mobile, AL) messaged using Signal – "So I guess I am taking full gear less weapons? Would rather have it and not need it." FBI documents indicate he brought the weapons and other Oath Keepers deposited them at the Comfort Inn. He'll plead guilty to "Conspiracy" and "Obstruction" - awaiting sentencing.

Jan 2, 2021. 18-year-old **Bruno Cua** (18, Milton, GA) wrote on Parler - "President Trump is calling us to FIGHT!"

Jan 2, 2021. 43-year-old Logan Grover (Erie, CO) wrote – "Sadly, I recognize that violence is highly likely." He'll plead guilty to "Parading" - awaiting sentencing.

Jan 3, 2021. 29-year-old Karol Chwiesiuk (Chicago, IL) sent a text message saying he was going to "save the nation" and that he was planning to "fuck up some commies."

Jan 3, 2021. Bennie (70) and Sandra Parker (62, Morrow, OH) were in contact with Jessica Watkins coordinating their trip. Watkins texted to Bennie Parker – "Weapons are ok now…" Parker texted back – "So I can bring my gun?"

Jan 3, 2021. Edward Spain (55, Chelsea, OK) posted on Parler - "PUBLIC SERVICE ANNOUNCEMENT: THE CIVIL WAR IN THE UNITED STATES IS EMMINENT!! ARM YOURSELVES WITH WEAPONS AND FIGHT FOR YOUR COUNTRY!!" He'll plead guilty to "Entering" – sentenced to 3 years' probation and 60 hours community service.

Jan 3, 2021. Matthew Webler (42, Decatur, GA) posts on FB - "I'll be in DC with my gun because if I'm wrong that's the only option left." He'll plead guilty to "Entering" – sentenced to 45 days' jail.

Jan 3, 2021. Air Force reservist Jamie Ferguson (44, Collinsville, VA) posted – "A Storm of Patriots will fight for the Republic, this will be an historic day…" She'll plead guilty to "Parading" - awaiting sentencing.

Jan 3, 2021. Three Percent member **Donald Hazard** (43, Hurst TX) on FB - "Check my new gear out helmet knuckle gloves and body armor as well"

Jan 4, 2021. QAnon supporter Cleveland Meredith (52, Hayesville, NC), on route to D.C., wrote – "5000rds of armor piercing green tip 5.563 in ma truk…We're gonna surround D.C. and slowly constrict." He'll plead guilty to "Threats" – sentenced to 28 months' jail and 3 years' probation.

Jan 4, 2021. Oath Keeper and Navy veteran Graydon Young (54, Englewood, FL) forwarded to Laura Steele an e-mail that said - "…we will also have well-armed and equipped QRF teams on standby…" He'll plead guilty to "Conspiracy" and "Obstruction"- awaiting sentencing.

Jan 4, 2021. **Garrett Miller** (34, Richardson, TX) before he embarked on his trip posted on FB – "Some crazy shit going to happen this week…civil war could start." Next day he noted that the last time he came to D.C. for a pro-Trump rally he "had lots of guns" with him.

Jan 4, 2021. Proud Boys fan Andrew Bennet (36, Columbia, MD) travelling to D.C. alone with a caravan of cars posted - "You better be ready chaos is coming and I will be in D.C. on 1/6/2021 fighting for my freedom!" He'll plead guilty to "Parading" – sentenced to 3 years' probation, 60 hours community service, and 90 days house arrest.

Jan 4, 2021. Jason Hyland (37, Frisco, TX) chartered a plane and while making arrangements texted – "I'm carrying a pocket knife." He advised fellow travelers who were bringing guns "…unload it at home and keep it out of sight…" He'll plead guilty to "Parading" – sentenced to 7 days' jails and $4,000 fine.

Jan 4, 2021. Jeremy Bertino (43, Belmont SC), a leader in the Proud Boys, wrote - "I say fuck it. Let's set it off…Drag them out by the fucking hair."

Jan 4, 2021. Justin Stoll (44, Wilmington, OH) posted – "You will get no quarters from me. Basically, if you are an enemy combatant, you will be shot on sight."

Jan 5, 2020. On his way to D.C. **Lucas Denney** (44, Mansfield, TX) posted on FB – "This is going to be huge. And it's going to be a fight…" He pleaded guilty to Assault with a Deadly Weapon and got 52 months' jail.

Jan 5, 2021. 3% member Derek Kinnison (Lake Elsinore, CA) chatted that he's bringing "medical kits, radios, multiple cans of bear spray, knives, flags, plates[,] goggles, [and] helmets." He'll be charged with "Conspiracy" and "Obstruction" among other crimes.

Jan 5, 2021. 3% member Ronald Mele (51, Temecula, CA)

texted his plans to bring a shotgun – ""Shorter the better. Mine will be able to be stashed under the seat. I'll bring it. 18" barrel." He'll be charged with "Conspiracy," "Obstruction," and being in a "Restricted Building".

Jan 5, 2021. Stephanie Baez (27, Orange, CA) posted on Instagram – "I just came out to Washington D.C. alone to fight antifa."

Jan 5, 2021. Thomas Conover (53, Kellar TX) wrote – "Shit storm is coming but that's what the democrats want." He'll plead guilty to "Parading" – sentenced to 3 years' probation, $2.500 fine, and 60 hours community service.

Jan 5, 2021. **Jeffrey Brown** (54, Irvine, CA) posted on Telegram - "This group will serve as the Comms for able bodied individuals that are going to D.C. on Jan 6. Many of us have not met before and we are all ready and willing to fight. We will come together for this moment that we are called upon." On Jan 6 he pepper sprayed officers.

Jan 5, 2021. On his way to Washington with his girlfriend, Dana Winn (45, Middleburg, FL) sent a video and referred to his girlfriend (Rachel Pert – also arrested) saying - "Got her flags, come with her flagpole, that way I can hit antifa in the head if need be…" Winn pleaded guilty to "Entering" – sentenced to 10 days' jail, 1 year probation, and 100 hours community service. Pert got no jail, 2 years' probation and 100 hours community service.

Jan 5, 2021. Kene Lazo (42, Norfolk, VA), one of the few Asians arrested, posted – "if shit hits the fan I will get some dead guys [sic] gear and guns if it comes down to it." He'll plead guilty to "Parading" – sentenced to 45 days' jail.

Jan 5, 2021. Russell Taylor (40, Ladera Ranch, CA) posted a photo showing his "gear" – 2 hatchets, a stun baton, and a knife. Later he spoke to the crowd and said - "We are free Americans and in these streets, we will fight and we will bleed before we allow our freedom to be taken from us." Charged with "Conspiracy", "Obstruction" and "Unlawful Possession of a Deadly Weapon," he's scheduled for a Jury trial.

Jan 5, 2021. According to FBI documents 20-year-old Caleb Berry (20, Tampa, FL) and other Oath Keepers dropped off weapons at the Comfort Inn Ballston Hotel in Arlington. He'll plead guilty to "Conspiracy" and "Obstruction" – awaiting sentencing.

Jan 5, 2021. Nicholas DeCarlo (30, Burleson, TX) who claimed he was a journalist, posted a video entitled "Twas the Night Before REVOLUTION!!!!" In the video he is walking around Washington with Nicholas Ochs, arrested for violent behavior.

Jan 5, 2021. 240-pound body builder and MMA fighter with prior arrest history **Scott Fairlamb** (43, Stockholm, NJ) wrote on FB the day before the riot – "Fate whispers to the warrior 'You cannot withstand the storm' and the warrior whispers back 'I am the storm.'" He'll plead guilty to "Assault" and "Obstruction" – sentenced to 41 months' jail and 3 years' probation.

Jan 5, 2021. High school PE teacher Kenneth Rader (54, Melbourn, Iowa) posted on FB – "I'm on my way to the front line. We are 1 day away from Civil War." He'll plead guilty to "Parading" – sentenced to 3 months' jail and 3 years' probation.

Jan 5, 2021. **John Wright** (54, Canton OH) - "WE ARE GOING TO HAVE TO FIGHT THE BLUE TOMORROW" "WE HAVE ENOUGH TO PUSH THRU" "WE ARE GOING IN AND DRAG THEM OUT" Shortly after midnight, he wrote – "THE FIRST MISTAKE THEY MAKE IN CHAMBERS WE ARE GOING IN AND DRAG THEM OUT." He'll plead guilty to "Civil Disorder" and "Obstruction" – awaiting sentencing.

Jan 6, 2021. **Guy Reffitt** (48, Wylie, TX), a leader of the 3% extremist group, in the morning posted - "As we oil our weapons. Hold our beer and watch this shit." Found guilty by a Jury of

"Obstruction" and 4 other charges and sentenced to 87 months' jail and 3 years' probation.

Jan 6, 2021. Samuel Fisher (35, Manhattan, NY) wrote - "1 Million Pissed off men with guns…bad idea. We aren't looking to fight or hurt anyone… but the odds that this is going to be solved any other way… is next to nothing." Later he wrote - "I'm Going To the parking garage super early," "Leaving s*** in there maybe except pistol…if it kicks off I got a Vest and My Rifle." He'll plead guilty to "Entering" – awaiting sentencing.

Jan 6, 2021. Before the riot, **Kenneth Thomas** (38, East Liverpool, OH) posted a video in which he said - "Right now, we got a whole [list] of people going to storm the Capitol." He was caught on camera pushing against police officers and punching and striking officers with his fist and forearm.

Jan 6, 2021. Before the riot MAGA caravan organizer **Clifford Mackrell** (20, Wellington, OH) posted on FB – "…it is out [sic] literal job as american's [sic] to kill the tyrannical government. Also fuck all news stations."

Jan 6, 2021. On his way to the riot, Jacob Wiedrich (23, Sandy, UT), using an alias, posted on SnapChat – "It's wartime…Charge… we die for Trump." He'll plead guilty to "Parading" – sentenced to 3 years' probation, 100 hours' community service, and 90 days' house arrest: no jail, no fine.

Jan 6, 2021. Brandon Fellows (27, Schenectady, NY) posted on FB – "And they know many of us had guns at our hotel rooms and vehicles…we just aren't pissed enough to kill the police or military. But we will fight them and make them retreat. Maybe things will get worse."

Jan 6, 2021. Christy Clark (44, Lewistown, PA) on her way to the Capitol posted on FB – "we r [sic] headed there now prepped [sic] for war."

These social media posts did not go un-noticed nor unreported. Here are some examples of intelligence gathered but not acted upon –

Dec 24, 2020. E-mail to Trump as reported by January 6 Committee (J6C) – Trump supporters are "armed and ready Mr. President...march into the chambers...make sure they know who to fear."

Dec 26, 2020. Secret Service e-mail as reported by J6C – "they will have a large enough group to march into D.C. armed and will outnumber the police so they can't be stopped. Their plan is to literally kill people. Please please take this tip seriously."

Dec 30, 2020. Secret Service e-mail as reported by J6C – "USMC is seeing a lot of violent rhetoric on Parler."

Dec 31, 2020. Secret Service Protective Intelligence Report – "President Trump supporters have proposed a movement to occupy Capitol Hill..."

Jan 4, 2021. CTS Intelligence Summary as reported by J6C – Trump supporters planning to "arm themselves and to engage in political violence at the event...invading the capitol building."

Jan 5, 2021. Secret Service e-mail as reported by J6C - "Right-wing groups...establishing 'quick reaction forces' in Virginia... Standing by at the ready should POTUS request assistance."

I know this section was long, but I thought it important to provide a glimpse into the mind-set of the participants, remembering that there are more people and more comments from the people already referenced. This was not a MAGA tourist event or a day at Disney World. Bear in mind, these are only the items discovered, so they represent "at least" in every case.

Overall, more than half of the people arrested for participating in the riot had some form of Violent Intention (VI) prior to the riot. The highest level of violent intent was found for the 200+ men arrested for violent behavior – 72%. This was followed by the non-violent men (60%) and the women (49%). Looking at the three factors being measured, wearing combat gear was most common for violent offenders (55%) followed by non-violent men (35%) and women (23%). Wearing a disguise was most common for women (27%) and non-violent men (25%) followed by violent offenders (20%). This reversal for violent offenders suggests that the people who came intent on violence were prepared to go all the way and were not afraid to be identified. Alternately, they may have assumed a disguise was unmanly. Finally, in terms of pre-riot social media posts, non-violent violent men outpolled the violent offenders and women (26% vs. 16% vs.11%).

Bear in mind that two of these measures (combat gear, disguise) are easily accessible from the documentation. The social media intent, on the other hand, is only discernible when the FBI quotes pre-riot behavior. On more than half the FBI reports, pre-riot behavior isn't mentioned, as the complaints focus on documenting riot behavior. This raises the possibility that social media intents to engage in violent behavior are much higher than assessed, but it's difficult to estimate how much under-reporting occurs. Taking this lack of evidence into consideration, it's highly likely that more than half the people arrested for the Jan 6 riot had violent intentions long before the date of the riot. In addition, the FBI list of wanted but yet unidentified capitol rioters has a substantial portion of people who cannot be identified because they wore gas masks or disguises.

When comparing violence intentioned (VI) rioters with the non-intentioned rioters among all the people who committed a violent offense, VI rioters came from smaller cities, were younger, less likely to be from higher SES groups, more likely to have experienced money problems, less likely to be registered to vote, and more likely to belong to an extremist group. They were more likely to be gun owners, more likely to be divorced, less likely to be homeowners though their homes were more likely to have higher estimated value. All things considered, the VI rioters are a less desirable group.

These data indicate that for half of the defendants, and very possibly more than half, violence was on the agenda for Jan 6. The premeditation for violence means that Jan 6 was not a rally gone badly, but a planned violent event. To check on this hypothesis, we can look at the extent to which rioters had prior arrest histories and the extent to which they belonged to extremist groups.

PRIOR ARREST HISTORY

Most of the people arrested on Jan 6 had prior arrest histories. For violent men, only 36% had a "clean record": 21% had prior convictions for assault (e.g., rape, domestic violence, assault) and 35% had prior convictions for major crimes not including assault (e.g., theft, larceny, forgery, weapons possession, drug manufacturing). The profile for non-violent men wasn't much different – 37% had no arrest record, 18% for assault, and 36% for major crimes except assault. Women were slightly less felonious – 37% with clean records, 15% with assault and 26% with major crimes except assault.

Considering the fact that more than 90% of the rioters were White, the percent with clean records is about half the expected rate. Another way to look at the statistics is to compare the percent of White people who commit violent crimes in general and the percent of White rioters who were arrested for violent crimes. According to the FBI, 4% of the four million Whites arrested in 2019 committed Part 1 violent crimes. On Jan 6, almost 30% of the White rioters were arrested for violent behavior. However you look at it, the White people who made up more than 90% of the rioters, were far more prone to violence than normal White people.

EXTREMIST GROUPS

Extremist groups are not necessarily violent, but among right-wing extremist groups, violence is an accepted strategy. They often align themselves with historical military images (e.g., American Revolutionary soldiers or Nazi Atomwaffen Divisions) to reinforce their violent actions, and often dress in military gear and adopt military language.

Social science research on violence and extremist groups is limited, but there are several studies which are informative. Gary Lafree and associates in 2018 found that within extremist groups, factors such as mental illness, lack of stable employment, prior arrest history, and radicalized peers were more important than marital status and education level in predicting violence. Interestingly, they found that leaders were less likely to act out even while appearing to be more mission oriented. Data from Profiles of Individual Radicalization in the United States suggests that violence in extremist groups is more common for young, male, unmarried, and unemployed or under-employed group members with histories of substance abuse or mental illness. Military experience, on the other hand was not a key factor.

We can assist further in the attempt to decide the extent to which the Jan 6 riot/insurrection was a rally gone badly or an intentional violent assault by determining the extent to which extremist groups were represented. We already know that at least half of the people came with some expectation for violence and that less than half the people had "clean records," and a substantial number had prior arrest records for assault, especially among the men where the rate was about 20% for assault and 35% for other major crimes.

Turning to January 6, about 30% of the rioters who were arrested had some connection to an extremist group, and some had connections to multiple groups. For women, the groups most represented were QAnon, anti-vaxxers, and Oath Keepers. For violent men it was Proud Boys, QAnon, and White Supremacists. For non-violent men, Proud Boys, Oath Keepers, and 3%ers.

Looking only at the more than 400 people who accepted pleas, the percent drops to 28% overall, and the most common groups are QAnon, Militia, and Proud Boys. In any event, a substantial number of the participants in the Jan 6 riot had ties to or were members of extremist groups, lending further credence to the idea that Jan 6 was a planned event in which violence was an intended process.

Extremists who were more represented among plea takers than among rioters were QAnon, GOP office holders and donors, and anti-vaxxers. These would seem to be the extremists with the least commitment to their mission. Extremists less represented among plea takers were 3%ers and White Supremacists. These would seem to be the hard-core extremists. The difference in total memberships suggests that people who accepted pleas were more inclined to belong to multiple groups, suggesting a lack of commitment to any particular group.

CHAPTER SUMMARY

By themselves, no one of the factors considered in this chapter would conclusively indicate that the Jan 6 event was a planned and violent affair. Neither wearing combat gear, carrying combat equipment, using disguises, anticipating violence on social media, prior arrest records, especially for violent behavior, and membership in extremist groups is a sine qua non for labeling the event as planned and violent. But when taken as a whole, the data is overwhelming. People who were prone to violent behavior and/or members of extremist groups known to be violent, came to D.C. on Jan 6 prepared for violence by bringing combat gear and equipment, using disguises to hide their identities, and indicating their desire to use violence in social media long before the event. These facts are vital when considering the sentences that were used. By understanding who the people were who came to D.C. on Jan 6 it's clear that for most people this was not a "MAGA tourist event". What exactly was it? If not a "MAGA tourist event" or a rally gone badly, was this action treason? An attempt to overthrow the government? Insurrection? Sedition? In the next chapter we'll explore in more depth the nature of the people who came to Washington on Jan 6 to shed more light on the situation.

THE RIOTERS

"Narcissistic symbiosis refers to the developmental wounds that make the leader-follower relationship magnetically attractive. The leader, hungry for adulation to compensate for an inner lack of self-worth, projects grandiose omnipotence—while the followers, rendered needy by societal stress or developmental injury, yearn for a parental figure. When such wounded individuals are given positions of power, they arouse similar pathology in the population that creates a "lock and key" relationship." **Dr. Brandon Lee**

There are several groups of rioters that can be analyzed – the entire population of 900+ who were arrested, the 400+ with plea agreements, and the 300+ who were sentenced (as of November 2022). These groups differ on several dimensions. For example, few of the people arrested for violent behavior have accepted plea agreements, and while many people with extremist ties have accepted pleas, members of the 3%ers and White Supremacists are disproportionately absent. This study focuses on the people sentenced, but first let's look at the entire cohort of rioters as of November 2022 –

THE RIOTERS' PROFILE

- 931 people charged, out of an estimated total of 3,000.

- Apart from misdemeanors, the most common charges were violence (236), destroying property (62), conspiracy (61), and theft (46).

- 457 agreed to pleas

- 300 were sentenced

- 11 cases dismissed, and 1 person found "not guilty"

- 796 (85%) men and 135 (15%) women

- 90%+ were White. The next largest ethnic groups were Hispanics, followed by Blacks and Asians.

- Median age for men = 38, women = 44.

- Median size town = 26,944. About 61% come from cities of 50,000 or less even though only 39% of the people in the U.S. live in smaller cities. 37% come from towns with less than 10,000 people.

- People came from 49 of the 50 states. On a per capita basis, the states with the biggest contributions (in order) were D.C., Pennsylvania, Montana, Virginia, and Ohio. The states least represented were North Dakota, Vermont, Louisiana, Nevada, Hawaii, Mississippi, Nebraska, South Dakota, Massachusetts, and Arkansas.

- 73% attended college and 40% graduated with a B.A. Less than 10% had advanced degrees.

- More than half the men and nearly 40% of the women experienced financial problems (e.g., liens, bankruptcies, closed businesses). Most of these problems were pre-Covid.

- Fewer than half owned their own homes, and the estimated median value of the homes they owned was under $200,000. A substantial number lived in mobile homes.

- About 12% of the men and 20% of the women used aliases on a regular basis.

- More than 60% of the participants were married. Women had the highest percent (80%+) followed by non-violent men (70%+) and violent men (60%+).

- About 16% of men and 4% of women had military backgrounds. Marines were over-represented and Navy and Air Force under-represented. The highest-ranking officer was a Lt. Col.

- About 8% had Police backgrounds including more than a dozen active.

- 30% had ties to extremist groups. The most common groups for men were Proud Boys, QAnon, and 3%ers. For women it was

QAnon and anti-vaxxers.

- More than half were registered Republicans and more than half of them didn't vote in 2020.

- The most common professions were blue collar workers (34%), small business owners (15%), and salespeople (7%). Unemployed, homeless, students, and retired people made up about 16% of the rioters.

- More than 40% of the men had prior arrest records and nearly 20% had prior arrests for assault. Women had over 60% with prior arrest records but only 15% for assault. 37% of the women's prior arrests were for traffic- related offenses, higher than non-violent or violent men (26%).

- Over 60% came to D.C. with combat gear and equipment, and/or disguises, and/or made comments on social media anticipating committing violence by shooting, killing, hanging, stabbing, blowing up, spraying, or otherwise harming Police and elected officials.

- More than 30% claimed they came to D.C. to protest the election.

- More than 30% came to D.C. with a relative, most commonly a spouse or a parent/child team, and least commonly a brother/sister team. In the case of husband/wife teams, more than 60% of the time both were arrested.

- Nearly 30% of the women came with their spouse. This was less true for non-violent men (10%) and violent men (14%).

- About 20% of the men who were arrested for violence came alone, while the figure for non-violent men was 17% and for women it was 4%.

- More than half the people charged for violence carried weapons. The most common weapons were sticks of any shape (25%), caustic spray (19%), on-site material like barricades and shields (18%), and guns or knives (6%). Overall, 19% of all rioters used a weapon.

- More than 100 of the 900+ people arrested were fired, suspended, resigned, or closed their business following their arrest. Punitive action was more common in fields like law enforcement, education, and public service

THE SENTENCED RIOTERS

The 300+ sentenced rioters ranged in age from 22 to 80 (median = 39). There were 82% men and 18% women. Among the men, 17% had a military background, mostly Army. Most were White (92%), followed by Hispanics, Blacks, and 1 each was from Lebanon and Vietnam. They came from towns with a median size of 24,533 people and half of the towns had fewer than 10,000 residents.

There were at least 11 couples (Bustle, Miller, Vinson, Getsinger, Schubert, Spencer, Pert/Winn, Wilson, Burress/Petit, Genco/Samsel, Gold/Strand,), 5 pairs of brothers (Cordon, Carrollo, Kukas, Quick, von Bernewitz) and 3 pairs of cousins (Bauer/Hemenway, Hiles/Horning, Bromley/Nix) all of whom were arrested. Even more disturbing, there were 4 parent and child combos where both were arrested (Buhler/Hardin, Grace, Johnson, Krzywicki/Levin). Almost half came with a friend, 13% came with a Spouse, 17% came with a relative, and 21% came alone.

The most common professions were Blue Collar worker (38%), Small Business Owner (14%), Salesperson (7%), Professionals (6%), or Management (5%): 9% were unemployed and 6% retired. More than 50% were registered Republicans, but 45% hadn't voted in 2020. The demographics for this group who were sentenced didn't differ significantly in most areas from the demographics for the entire group of 400+ people who agreed to pleas. Sentenced people had more unemployed, fewer Marines, and came from cities half as large as the un-sentenced plea takers.

The defendants were arrested between Jan. 6, 2021, and July 12, 2022 (median = Dec 2, 2021). The median time between arrest and plea agreement was 221 days and between plea agreement and sentencing was 100 days, for a total of 321 days.

Among the sentenced people, 27% were associated with extremist groups, most notably QAnon (10%) followed by Proud Boys (5%) and Anti-vaxxers (3%). At least 26% came in combat gear or with combat equipment, 28% used disguises, and at least 23% posted intentions to commit violence at the Jan 6 event. At least 55% had one or more of these Violence Indicators and 19% had two or more.

Nearly 60% had prior arrest histories (e.g., child endangerment, drug possession, weapons possession, drug manufacturing, forcible entry) and 18% for assault (e.g., domestic violence, sexual battery, attempted murder). Many of these people had multiple charges against them and some had already done time in jail. Only 44% had "clean records." Criminal background records were difficult to obtain so it's likely that there are more people and more charges.

The characteristics of the rioters are important to document because one of the major elements to consider in sentencing the defendants is their character. Almost every "Government's Sentencing Memorandum" has a section called "The History and Character of the Offender" in which DOJ prosecutors discussed issues such as marital status, arrest record, employment, and compliance with conditions, and upon reviewing these issues, the DOJ prosecutors make a recommendation as to the type and severity of punishment appropriate.

As we consider the sentences, these data are important to keep in mind.

THE CHARGES

"Violence is the end product of a long process, so prevention is key. Structural violence, or inequality, is the most potent stimulant of behavioral violence. And reducing inequality in all forms—economic, racial and gender—will help toward preventing violence." **Dr. Brandon Lee**

Many people wonder why the rioters have not been charged with "treason." Instead, almost 90% have been charged with misdemeanors like "Parading, Demonstrating, Picketing in a Capitol Building" (73%), "Entering and Remaining in a Restricted Building or Grounds" (12%), and "Disorderly and Disruptive Conduct in a Restricted Building" (3%). Let's examine the charges that could be and the charges that are being used.

TREASON

Treason (18 USC 2381) is the act of betraying one's own country by attempting to overthrow the government through waging war against the state or materially aiding its enemies. It carries a penalty of death, a fine of no less than $10,000, and makes it impossible to hold office. According to most legal scholars, the words "waging war" make it difficult to apply treason to the Jan 6 riot/insurrection.

Treason was used following World War II to charge "Axis Sally" and "Tokyo Rose" and several other Americans who gave aid to the Germans and Japanese. They served decades in jail, and most were ultimately released or pardoned. Execution hasn't been used to punish a traitor since Mary Surratt was convicted for her alleged participation in the conspiracy to assassinate Abraham Lincoln.

REBELLION OR INSURRECTION

Rebellion or Insurrection (18 USC 2383) has no definition of the specific acts, thus making it difficult to charge anyone. It carries the same penalty as treason. Here is the specific text -

"Whoever incites, sets on foot, assists, or engages in any rebellion or insurrection against the authority of the United States or the laws thereof, or gives aid or comfort thereto, shall be fined under this title or imprisoned not more than ten years, or both; and shall be incapable of holding any office under the United States."

To charge, much less convict, anyone of "rebellion" or "insurrection" one must depend on definitions found outside the law. Rebellion is defined as "an act of violent or open resistance to an established government or ruler" and Insurrection is defined as "a violent uprising against an authority or government." By either definition, the Jan 6 participants surely could be charged with either of these offenses. After all, over 200 people were charged with violent acts.

Rebellion and Insurrection differ from Treason because they do not require allegiance to the government. They also differ from Sedition or Seditious Conspiracy because these charges do not require any organized resistance. But arguments that this behavior is covered by the First Amendment ignore the violent aspect required for the charges to be made. Despite the obvious fact that rebellion and insurrection can be charged, they are rarely used. Instead, the Government tends to charge people with specific violent acts (e.g., assault).

OVERTHROW OF GOVERNMENT

18 USC 2385 addresses a lengthy list of attempts to overthrow or destroy any branch of the government "by force or violence or by assassination." It carries a maximum 20-year sentence along with 5 years' denial of government employment.

In 2020 as the elections drew near, then Attorney General Barr speculated about using the charge "overthrowing the U.S. government" against Antifa and other anti-Trump groups. It wasn't used, but it was employed pre- and post-World War II against Socialists and Communists.

SEDITIOUS CONSPIRACY

The charge "seditious conspiracy" (18 USC 2384) is more easily applied than the charges already discussed. It's defined under federal law as –

> *"If two or more persons in any State or Territory, or in any place subject to the jurisdiction of the United States, conspire to overthrow, put down, or to destroy by force the Government of the United States, or to levy war against them, or to oppose by force the authority thereof, or by force to prevent, hinder, or delay the execution of any law of the United States, or by force to seize, take, or possess any property of the United States contrary to the authority thereof, they shall each be fined under this title or imprisoned not more than twenty years, or both."*

The charge of seditious conspiracy is not levied often, but it has been used successfully several times in the last century, notably in 1936 and 1980 against Puerto Rican nationalists, and in 1995 against a Muslim cleric. Penalties ranged from 10 to 90 years.

The social media posts by many of the Jan 6 rioters include comments that are consistent with "opposing by force the authority thereof, or by force to prevent, hinder, or delay the execution of any law of the United States…" The "laws" in this case would be Article II, Section 1, Clause 2 of the Constitution and, more particularly, the Twelfth Amendment which sets out how the Electoral College functions. The "force" in this case is the presence of weapons, theft and destruction or property, and the assault upon the Police documented in thousands of hours of video tape.

For example, according to the FBI -

- On Dec. 29, 2020, George Tenney from South Carolina, wrote - *"It's starting to look like we may siege the capital building and congress if the electoral votes don't go right…"*
- On Jan. 2021, Navy veteran and Oath Keeper leader Thomas Caldwell wrote "…*they have morphed into pure evil even blatantly rigging an election and paying off the political caste. We must smite them now and drive them down."*
- On Jan 6. 2021, shortly after midnight, 54-years old John Wright from Canton Ohio wrote – *"THE FIRST MISTAKE THEY MAKE IN CHAMBERS WE ARE GOING IN AND DRAG THEM OUT."*

These and countless other evidence gathered by the FBI show that at least some of the rioters intended to use force and intended to "prevent, hinder, or delay the execution" of the law that day. Had they simply said what they said, their musing would be protected by the First Amendment. By going beyond speech into violent acts, the freedom of speech defense falls by the wayside.

The DOJ ignored "seditious conspiracy" until nearly a year after Jan 6, but they did cite 54 people for "conspiracy," Thomas Caldwell, mentioned above, being one of them. The conspiracy charge (18 USC 371) carries a 5-year maximum prison term, considerably less than the 20 years associated with "seditious conspiracy." It also allows fines up to $500,000. Neither treason, seditious conspiracy, overthrow, nor insurrection were used by the DOJ in 2021. The bottom line is that the DOJ has avoided using more serious charges. Let's see what they did do.

ACTUAL CHARGES

The 400+ rioters with plea agreements originally were charged with over a dozen different complaints, but following plea agreements, the charges were reduced to only a few, the most common being "Parading" (72%), "Entering" (54%), and "Disorderly" (49%). Here are the definitions and sentences for the most common charges used.

MISDEMEANOR CHARGES COMMONLY USED FOR JAN 6 DEFENDANTS		
Charge	**US Code**	**Class & Max Jail Time**
Parading	40 USC 5104 e 2 G	6 months' jail, $5,000 fine
Entering	18 USC 1752 a 1 and 2	1 year jail, $100,000 fine, 12 months' probation.
Disorderly	40 USC 5104 e 2 D	6 months' jail, $5,000 fine
Violent Entry	40 USC 5104 e 2 G	6 months' jail, $5000 fine

The difference between whether the Disorderly and Entering crimes are a Misdemeanor or Felony depends on whether "a deadly or dangerous weapon or firearm" was involved or if the crime "results significant bodily injury." For Obstruction, an 8-year penalty can be assessed if the crime involves "domestic terrorism." For Assault, an 8-year penalty can be assessed if the crime accompanies another felony, and 20 years if a "deadly or dangerous weapon" is used or "bodily injury" occurs. For Conspiracy, for a felony there's a 5 years' maximum jail time. If it involves a Misdemeanor, the maximum penalty is the same as for the Misdemeanor.

FELONY CHARGES COMMONLY USED FOR JAN 6 DEFENDANTS		
Charge	US Code	Class & Max Jail Time
Obstruction	18 USC 1512 c 2	20 years' jail, $250,000, fine, 36 months' probation
Assault	18 USC 111 a 1	8 years' jail, $250,000 fine, 36 months' probation.
Assault with Deadly Weapon	18 USC 111 a b	20 years' jail
Interstate Communication of Threats	18 USC 875 c	5 years' jail
Civil Disorder	18 USC 231 a 3	5 years' jail, 8 years if terrorism
Theft of Government Property	18 USC 641	10 years' jail, 1 year if value <$1000
Conspiracy	18 USC 371	5 years' jail, $250,000 fine

In moving from original to final charges, the DOJ reduced an average of 4+ charges per person to a single charge and removed the felony from over a dozen defendants. This process will be addressed more fully later.

CHAPTER SUMMARY

Defendants could be charged with a multitude of offenses ranging from major felonies to minor misdemeanors. The differences are substantial – maximum prison time ranges from 6 months to 20 years and fines can range from $0 to $500,000. In addition, the more serious charges can prohibit the felon from voting or holding federal office.

THE JUDGES

"I am quite aware that there are people who are criticizing us for not prosecuting sufficiently and others who are complaining that we are prosecuting too harshly. This is, you know, part of the territory for any prosecutor in any case, I have great confidence in the prosecutors who are doing these cases." **AG Garland**

In the nearly two years following the Jan 6 riot, over 300 people were sentenced. A total of 21 Judges were employed, most of whom sat for at least two cases. Most of the Judges had been appointed by Obama (8) or Trump (4), followed by Clinton (2), Bush (2), Reagan (2) and Biden (3). They were mostly White men.

JUDGE'S SCORECARD

The Judges' rulings and characteristics are noted in the tables on the following pages. The first figure shows their profile. The second figure shows their performance through November 2022 for the first 300 cases where the defendants pleaded.

There are several surprising results. Judges accepted DOJ recommendations in only 11% of the cases while in 77% of the cases, Judges gave more lenient sentences than recommended. Leniency was found for both Democrat and Republican appointees though more severity was more associated with Obama-appointed Judges.

CAPITOL RIOT JUDGES' PROFILES (NOVEMBER 2022)

	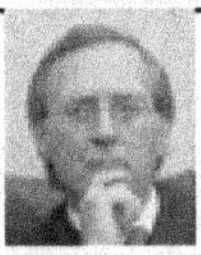	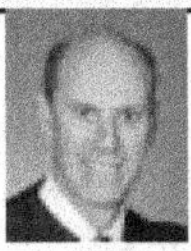	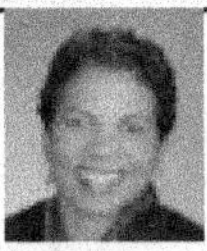	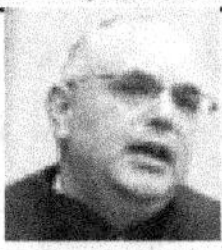	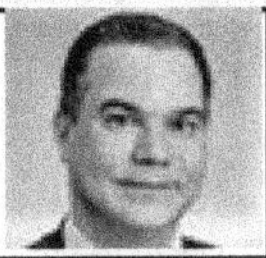	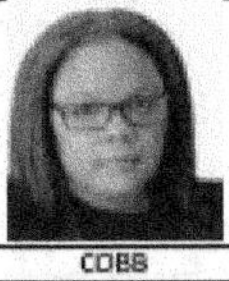
NAME	BATES	BOASBERG	CHUTKAN	CONTRERAS	COOPER	COBB
APPOINTED	BUSH – 2001	OBAMA – 2011	OBAMA – 2014	OBAMA – 2012	OBAMA – 2014	BIDEN - 2021
AGE	75	58	59	58	55	42
SEX	M	M	S	M	M	F
RACE	WHITE	WHITE	JAMAICAN	CUBAN	BLACK	BLACK
SCHOOL	UNIV MD	YALE	UNIV PA	UNIV PENN	STANFORD	HARVARD
NOTES	AUSA	Private practice	Private practice		Private practice	Public Defender

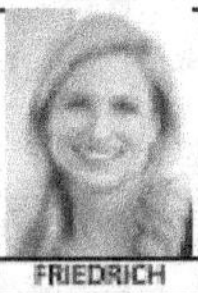

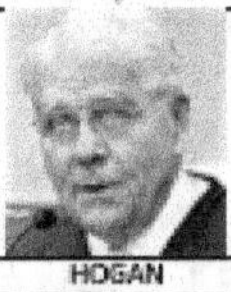

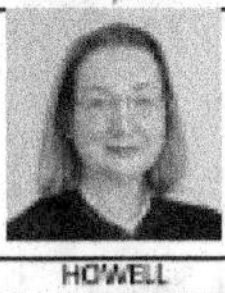

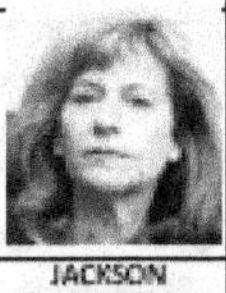

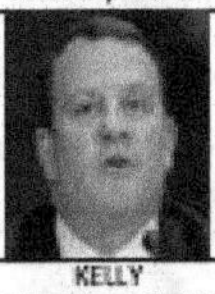

NAME	FRIEDRICH	HOGAN	HOWELL	JACKSON	KELLY
APPOINTED	TRUMP – 2017	REAGAN – 1982	OBAMA – 2010	OBAMA – 2011	TRUMP – 2015
AGE	54	83	54	57	52
SEX	F	M	F	F	M
RACE	WHITE	WHITE	WHITE	WHITE	WHITE
SCHOOL	YALE	GEORGETOWN	COLUMBIA	HARVARD	GEORGETOWN
NOTES	Counsel W Bush	Private practice	Private practice	Private practice	Fed prosecutor

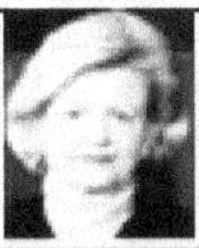

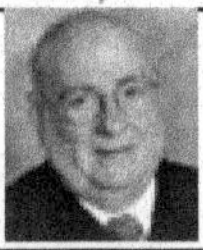

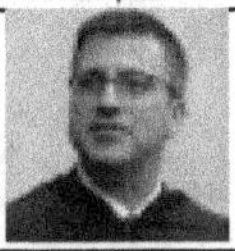

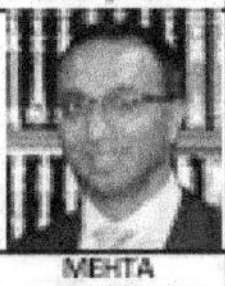

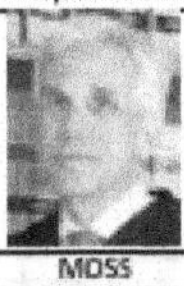

NAME	KOLLAR	LAMBERTH	MCFADDEN	MEHTA	MOSS
APPOINTED	CLINTON – 1997	REAGAN – 1987	TRUMP – 2017	OBAMA – 2014	OBAMA – 2014
AGE	78	68	43	50	60
SEX	F	M	M	M	M
RACE	WHITE	WHITE	WHITE	INDIAN	WHITE
SCHOOL	CATHOLIC U	UNIV TEXAS	UNIV VA	UNIV VA	YALE
NOTES	Commerce Dept	Capt. Army JAG	AUSA	Private practice	Private practice

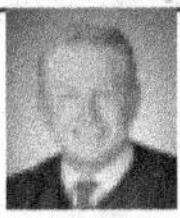

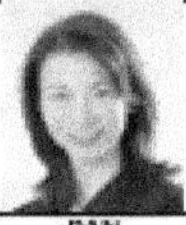

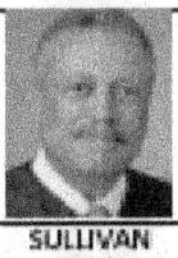

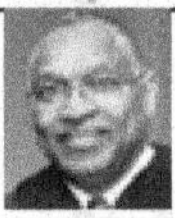

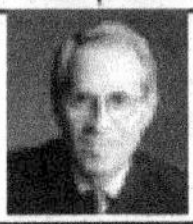

NAME	NICHOLS	PAN	SULLIVAN	WALTON	FRIEDMAN
APPOINTED	TRUMP -2019	BIDEN – 2021	CLINTON – 1994	BUSH – 2001	CLINTON – 1994
AGE	51	55	75	72	78
SEX	M	F	M	M	M
RACE	WHITE	ASIAN	BLACK	BLACK	WHITE
SCHOOL	UNIV CHICAGO	STANFORD	HOWARD	AMERICAN U	STATE U BUFFALO
NOTES	C Thomas Clerk		Private practice		private practice

JUDGES' SCORECARD – 300 PEOPLE SENTENCED (NOV 2022)

NAME	CONTRERAS (16)	BATES (7)	MCFADDEN (17)	BOASBERG (15)	HOGAN (18)
APPOINTED	OBAMA	BUSH	TRUMP	OBAMA	REAGAN
LENIENT	100%	100%	94%	100%	83%
JAIL TIME	0%	17%	31%	69%	47%
% FINED	60%	67%	63%	15%	20%
% COM SERV	88%	100%	53%	73%	33%
NAME	LAMBERTH (19)	MEHTA (12)	FRIEDRICH (23)	KELLY (11)	COOPER (23)
APPOINTED	REAGAN	OBAMA	TRUMP	TRUMP	OBAMA
LENIENT	63%	100%	96%	100%	91%
JAIL TIME	67%	25%	5%	30%	56%
% FINED	33%	8%	30%	20%	50%
% COM SERV	5%	92%	65%	64%	26%
NAME	NICHOLS (16)	WALTON (10)	JACKSON (17)	HOWELL (30)	KOLLAR (9)
APPOINTED	TRUMP	BUSH	OBAMA	OBAMA	CLINTON
LENIENT	81%	70%	81%	80%	56%
JAIL TIME	56%	56%	42%	59%	67%
% FINED	0%	89%	42%	37%	0%
% COM SERV	69%	60%	41%	17%	11%
NAME	MOSS (12)	CHUTKAN (19)	FRIEDMAN (7)	PAN (6)	SULLIVAN (8)
APPOINTED	OBAMA	OBAMA	CLINTON	BIDEN	CLINTON
LENIENT	75%	26%	43%	83%	0%
JAIL TIME	29%	100%	33%	83%	100%
% FINED	14%	8%	33%	33%	13%
% COM SERV	67%	58%	83%	83%	100%

Calculations except jail & fines for Misdemeanor cases only. Data from pleading cases only (no bench/jury).

https://www.amazon.com/Jan-Justice-Department-Betrayed-Nation/dp/B09PMBSWSN/

JUDGE'S COMMENTS

Judges often showed their inclinations in their statements during the trial and upon sentencing. Here is a collection of comments by Judges when sentencing defendants.

Judges For The Defendant

Almost all of the rulings by Trump-appointee Judge **Trevor McFadden** were in favor of defendants and less than the DOJ recommended. That's congruent with his comments -

"The US Attorney's Office would have more credibility if it was even-handed in its concern about riots and mobs in the city... In my experience as a judge and a former prosecutor, it's almost unheard of for someone who is a first-time offender to get jail time for a nonviolent misdemeanor."

Judges For The Prosecution

Obama-appointed Judge **Tanya Chutkan** almost always added time to the recommendations of the DOJ. That's congruent with her comments -

"...walked away with probation and a slap on the wrist it wouldn't deter anyone from trying what he did again because the country is watching to see what the consequences are for something that has not ever happened in this country before, for actions and crimes that undermine the rule of law and our democracy."

Words Don't Match Actions

68-year-old Reagan-appointed **Royce Lamberth** ruled for the defendant most of the time, but his words suggest otherwise -

"… the attempt of some congressman to rewrite history that these were tourists walking through the capitol is utter nonsense. This wasn't a peaceful demonstration… it wasn't an accident that it turned violent."

On Jan 28, 2022, Lamberth revealed his true nature when refusing to follow the DOJ recommendation for incarceration and instead sentenced Justin McAuliffe to probation, saying "A judge has to have mercy."

Obama-appointed **Judge Beryl Howell** mostly ruled in favor of the defendant, yet her comments make it sound like she would do otherwise – "Let me make my view clear: The rioters were not mere protesters." When sentencing Jack Griffith she said - "This is a muddled approach by the government. I'm trying to make sense of the government's position here. The damage to the reputation of our democracy, which is usually held up around the world … that reputation suffered because of Jan. 6"

Obama-appointed **Judge Boasberg** is like Howell: remarks suggest punitive actions, but the rulings always went to the defendant. Sentencing Andrew Bennett he said - "The cornerstone of our democratic republic is the peaceful transfer of power after elections. What you and others did on January 6 th was nothing less than an attempt to undermine that system of government."

Reagan-appointee Judge **Thomas Hogan** ruled 81% in favor of the defendant, but he'd like people to think he's not on their side. When sentencing Robert Reeder he said - "It's become evident to me in the riot cases … that many of the defendants who are pleading guilty are not truly accepting responsibility. They seem to me to be trying to get this out of the way as quickly and as inexpensively as possible and stating whatever they have to say in guilty pleas and hoping to get probation and leave." It he honestly believed that he probably wouldn't rule in favor of the people whom he accuses of lying to him.

Obama-appointed Judge **Amy Jackson** joins the list of Judges who say one thing but behave in another way – 81% of her 16 rulings went to the defendant. Here are her comments –

"He is not a political prisoner. We are not here today because he supported former President Trump. He was an enthusiastic participant in an effort to subvert the electoral process."

Sentencing Russel Peterson she said - "It was sickening, it was horrifying, and it was utterly inconsistent with what this country stands for, and I'm concerned that there's an ongoing harm to what our democracy is supposed to be...and we don't know if it's replicable or not, because we really don't know yet if things will return to the way they were, or if a disorderly, violent reaction to elections is now an acceptable option to a large segment of the population."

Quite frankly, most of the federal Judges sound like politicians, pandering to the crowd while doing the opposite. Because no one keeps track of what they're doing, they get away with it. I may not like Judge McFadden's tendency to rule in favor of the defendants, but at least he owns his biases. From a different POV, Judge Chutkan does the same.

RULINGS AND APPOINTMENTS

There is no clear relationship between Trump vs. Obama appointed Judges and Defendant-oriented decisions – 60 of the Trump-appointees' 67 decisions (90%) went in favor of the Defendants, while 113 of the 142 (80%) decisions by Obama appointees were equally lenient. Older Judges (Reagan, Bush or Clinton appointees) tended to be less lenient (54%). Biden appointees were almost as lenient as Trump appointees – 8 of 9 decisions (89%) were less than the DOJ recommended.

When Judges took away jail time, their typical response was to add probation, followed by house arrest, community service, and occasionally add to the recommended fine (fine amounts could be as high as $9,000). Most often jail time would be taken away completely (e.g., Vinson, Griffith, Torrens, Gruppo, Croy, Stotts, K. Cordon, Abual-Ragheb, Nelson, Markofski, Marquez), but occasionally it was simply reduced. For example, Paul Hodgkins went from 18 to 8 months, Scott Fairlamb from 44 to 41 months, Jacob Chansley from 51 to 41 months, Derek Jancart and Eric Rau from 4 months to 45 days.

CHAPTER SUMMARY

Here are the main points covered in this chapter –

- In only 11% of the rulings, Judges accepted the DOJ recommendations. When they varied, Judges gave more lenient sentences than the DOJ recommended in 77% of the cases

- High leniency was found for Trump, Biden, and Obama appointees, though less for older Judges appointed by Reagan, Bush, or Clinton.

- More severity was more associated with Obama-appointed Judges, but Republican Judges did occasionally hand down a more severe sentence.

- Almost all the Judges spoke as if they viewed the defendants as insurrectionists, yet most Judges ruled in favor of defendants and handed out lenient sentences, putting only half the defendants in jail and those in jail with a median sentence of only 45 days.

THE SENTENCES

"AG Garland's speech was as empty as legal analysts expected it would be—full of entirely proper ideals that DOJ is not living up to where the rubber meets the road." **Seth Abramson, Jan 5, 2022**

GENERAL

In evaluating the DOJ treatment of Jan 6 defendants it's important to consider the general way things work and have a baseline.

The "Principles of Federal Prosecution", updated as recently as 2018, sets forth guidelines that DOJ prosecutors should follow, and understanding the relevant passages will be helpful.

9-27.300 – "Once the decision to prosecute has been made, the attorney for the government should charge and pursue the most serious, readily provable offenses. By definition, the most serious offenses are those that carry the most substantial guidelines sentence, including mandatory minimum sentences.'"

9-27.430 – "If a prosecution is to be concluded pursuant to a plea agreement, the defendant should be required to plead to a charge or charges: 1. That is the most serious readily provable charge consistent with the nature and extent of his/her criminal conduct; 2.That has an adequate factual basis; 3. That makes likely the imposition of an appropriate sentence and order of restitution, if appropriate, under all the circumstances of the case; and 4.That does not adversely affect the investigation or prosecution of others."

More than 90% of misdemeanor cases brought by the federal government are settled through plea agreements. In the federal system Judges are excluded from the plea process, and they are not necessarily bound by the Prosecutors' recommendations. The Prosecutor must inform the Defendant of the statutory requirements of the crime (e.g., maximum sentences) and the guidelines used in sentencing, but Judges are not bound to conform to the recommendations, only to the requirements. Defense attorneys are allowed to produce their own sentencing recommendations, and often do.

In nearly every case federal Judges impose either incarceration and/or probation. In only about a fifth of the cases are there minimal required sentences (e.g., drug trafficking). Prosecutors can ask for and Judges can also impose financial penalties (fines, restitution, and special assessments)

The average jail time in federal cases is 52 months, but in cases that don't involve a mandatory minimum sentence, the average is 28 months. For those people who are imprisoned, 86% received supervised release, with an average of 47 months. Overall, 88% of federal prisoners receive jail only sentences and a further 7% get probation only.

Most misdemeanors at the federal level are managed through the plea system, but some go to trial and at trial most cases are dismissed. The median number of days from filing to disposition in plea cases is slightly more than 200. In FY 2016, of the 5,753 misdemeanors at the federal level, 36% went to jail, 34% got probation only, 21% got fine only, and 9% got a suspended sentence. The median jail sentence was 6 months, and the median probation time was 12 months. For violent felonies, 93% went to jail, 3% got probation only, 3% got a suspended sentence, and less than 1% got a fine only. People convicted or disorderly conduct at the felony level went to jail 82% of the time, 12% probation only, and 6% suspended sentences.

Looking at the extent to which Judges follow guidelines in sentencing, in 2021, 68% were within guidelines. For those that fell outside the guidelines, 89% were in favor of the defendant with an average sentence reduction of 26%. Only 11% were in favor of the Prosecution and the average sentence enhancement was 60%.

SPECIFIC

Having looked at the way things work in general for federal prosecutions, we can turn to the Jan 6 event. For the specific crimes at the Capitol the DOJ has special 9-point guidance that is reproduced below–

"This Court, in determining a fair and just sentence on this spectrum, should look to a number of critical factors, including: (1) whether, when, and how the defendant entered the Capitol building; (2) whether the defendant engaged in any violence or incited violence; (3) whether the defendant engaged in any acts of destruction; (4) the defendant's reaction to acts of violence or destruction; (5) whether during or after the riot, the defendant destroyed evidence; (6) the length of the defendant's time inside the building, and exactly where the defendant traveled; (7) the defendant's statements in person or on social media; (8) whether the defendant cooperated with, or ignored, law enforcement; and (9) whether the defendant otherwise exhibited evidence of remorse or contrition. While these factors are not exhaustive or dispositive, they help to place each individual defendant on a spectrum as to their fair and just punishment."

Keep the general and specific factors in mind as we move forward.

To determine the extent of the strength of the sentences, I conducted a study of the people sentenced as of November 2022. As of that date, 900+ of the estimated 3,000 defendants had been arrested, 400+ had entered into plea agreements and over 300 had been sentenced.

METHODOLOGY

The methodology was straight-forward. Read the Government's Sentencing Memorandums and compare them with the Judges' rulings. Sometimes it wasn't always clear what the sentencing recommendation was. For example, in the case of Edward Hemenway the Prosecutor Elizabeth Kelley began by saying "For the reasons set forth herein, the government requests that this Court sentence defendant Edward E. Hemenway, II to 30 days' incarceration and $500 restitution." At the conclusion, she wrote – "Balancing these factors, the government recommends that this Court sentence Edward Hemenway to three months home confinement, followed by a three-year period of probation to include 60 hours of community service, and $500 restitution." Did she or did she not recommend incarceration?

Less befuddled, but still not exactly clear, is the recommendation of Prosecutor Michael Friedman in the case of Troy Smocks. Friedman wrote – "we respectfully suggest that the Court impose a term of imprisonment at the low end of the Sentencing Guidelines range, followed by three years of supervised release with conditions" without providing the guidelines. If you searched through the 8-page document you'll find buried this comment – "The parties agreed that the Estimated Guidelines Range is either 8-14 months of imprisonment (if Criminal History Category II) or 10-16 months of imprisonment (if Criminal History Category III)." So, not only are the guidelines not alongside the sentencing recommendation, where they are, it's not really clear what they are.

Sometimes the memorandum began with one recommendation and ended with a different one. For example, in sentencing Robert Palmer, prosecutor Robert Juman wrote – "…

the government requests that this Court sentence Robert Scott Palmer to 63 months' incarceration, three years of supervised release, $2,000 in restitution, and the mandatory $100 special assessment," but at the conclusion, 38 pages later, Juman wrote "...the government recommends that the Court impose a sentence of imprisonment of 63 months, which is the low point of the Guidelines range..." So, which is it? Does he get the 63 months or the 63 months plus probation, plus fines? These types of unclear comments made the analysis less than straight-forward, but thankfully, the confusions over recommendations were the exception. The fact that they exist, and are not rare, is a testament to the less than stellar job being done by the DOJ.

Not all sentences could be easily classified as either in favor of the defendant or the prosecution or neutral. For example, in the case of 35-year-old Sean Cordon who was arrested along with his brother, the DOJ asked for 36 months' probation, 3 months' house arrest, 60 hours community service, and a $500 fine. Trump-appointed Judge McFadden reduced probation from 36 to 2 months, threw out the house arrest and the community service, but bumped the fine from $500 to $4,500. Or take 80-year-old Gary Wickersham, a retired machine operator from West Chester Pennsylvania. The DOJ asked for 36 months' probation, 4 months' house arrest, 60 hours of community service, and a $500 fine. Reagan-appointed Judge Lamberth kept the probation, reduced the house arrest from 4 to 3 months, dropped the community service, but bumped the fine from $500 to $2,510. These types of mixed sentences were rare, and when they occurred, they were classified as "neutral." There were only a few of these types of decisions, and most "neutral" ratings refer to cases in which DOJ recommendations and Judge rulings were equal.

Generally speaking, any sentence that eliminated jail and replaced it with other elements was judged to be in favor of the Defendant. In a similar fashion, any sentence that reduced jail time regardless of whether it increased community service or a fine, was judged as being in favor of the defendant. Agreement between raters was more than 90% which in social science research is considered excellent. Nonetheless, it is not merely the judgment by itself but the judgement in relationship to the person. Home arrest is more of a punishment for a 30-year-old single man in NYC than it is for an 80-year-old man living in a small town in rural New Hampshire during a Pandemic.

OVERALL RESULTS: PLEADING

This section looks only at the 300+ people who pleaded and were sentenced. There is a separate chapter on Jury and Bench trials, and also a Chapter looking at Women and Non-Whites.

The results of the sentencing can be looked at in several ways, since there are at least five possible sentences (jail time, probation, fines, community service, and house arrest), and even among these sentences there are variations. For example, incarceration may be to a prison, a jail, or a "community correctional facility." It may be continuous or intermittent (e.g., on weekends). The differences are not insubstantial. Financial charges could be restitution, a fine, or an assessment. Moreover, Judges rarely gave a single penalty; more often, 2 or 3 penalties were combined, and sometimes 4 were used.

In the case of the 300+ defendants sentenced as of November 2022…

- 85% received probation (median 24 months, range 2 to 60).
- 55% received jail time (median 45 days, range 10 to 2,580 days).
- 54% received community service (median 60 hours, range 50 to 250).
- 55% received jail time (median 45 days, range 10 to 2,580 days).

- 28% received a fine (average $2,169, range $742 to $9,500).
- 28% received house arrest (median 62 days, range 30 to 120).

On average, defendants got 3 elements, the most common being (a) probation + fine + community service, (b) probation + fine + community service + house arrest, and (c) probation + fine + house arrest. Defendants sent to jail rarely got either house arrest or community service.

Jail Time

Because of the difficulty in trying to determine whether each of these five elements are restrictive, this first analysis focuses on jail time alone. It's easy to say whether 14 days is better or worse than 120 days, and equally easy to say that jail time is the most punitive option.

It was already noted that only 53% of the people sentenced got any jail time. One of the reasons that so few people got jail time is that several times Judges ignored the recommendations of the DOJ. For example, in the case of 25-year-old Jack Griffith from Gallatin Tennessee who pleaded guilty to "Parading", the DOJ asked for 3 months' jail, but Judge Howell gave him no jail time and instead gave him 36 months' probation, $500 "restitution", and 90 days' house arrest. Or consider 25-year-old Felipe Marquez from Florida, whom the FBI say drove alone to D.C. with a gun in his car. He pleaded guilty to "Disorderly". The DOJ asked for 4 months' jail, but Judge Contreras gave him 3 months' home confinement with mental health treatment and 18 months' probation.

Other examples in which the DOJ asked for jail time, but the Judges rejected their recommendations include Rasha Abual-Ragbeh, Kevin Cordon, Gary Edwards, Jack Griffith, Leonard

Gruppo, Abram Markofski, Anthony Mariotto, David Mish, Brandon Nelson, Jordan Stotts, Eric Torrens, Israel Tutrow, and Lori Vinson. Thus, well over a dozen people got a "get out of jail free" card. In contrast, the number of people that the DOJ didn't recommend for jail time whom the Judges sent to jail was very few (e.g., Donna Bissey, Matthew Mazzocco, Brandon and Stephanie Miller, Dana Winn). When Judges added jail time the average was only 20 days. When Judges went in the other direction, taking away jail time, the average difference was 45 days.

The table summarizes the results for the people who received jail time for Parading. Some notable observations –

- Males got slightly more average jail time than females, but median jail time was almost equal. Overall, no differences
- The average jail time was significantly less than the potential maximum sentence of 180 days. In fact, only 2 of the 188 people sentenced for parading got 180 days, and they were both men (Curzio and Dresch).
- The medians are about equal, but women get less average jail time, and the range is very different. For women the range is very truncated and trends toward the low side.

JAIL TIME FOR PARADING – WHITE MALES V FEMALES					
	Total Number (Jailed)	%	Median Length (Days)	Avg. Length (Days)	Range
White Males	150 (59)	39%	30	72	7-180
White Females	38 (16)	42%	25.5	36	10-90
Total	188 (75)	40%	30	41	7-180

If anyone were found guilty of parading the maximum prison sentence was 180 days. Looking at the sentences recommended by the DOJ, the average time dropped to 27 days. Once the Judges took their turn, the average went up to 46 days.

Disparities

Judgements for the same crime for similar defendants have not always been consistent. In several cases the Defense attorneys argued this point. In the case of Brittany Dillon, her attorney pointed to judgments for Jessica Bustle, Danielle Doyle, and Valerie Ehrke when he argued against home confinement. Let's compare –

SENTENCE DISPARITY AMONG FOUR WOMEN					
DEFENDANT (JUDGE)	JAIL	PR	FINE	HA	COMM SERV
Dillon (Friedrich)	0	36	$0	2	0
Bustle (Hogan)	0	24	$0	2	40
Doyle (McFadden)	0	2	$3,000	0	0
Ehrke (Friedman)	0	36	$0	0	120
PR=Probation (Months), HA=Home Arrest (Days), CS= Community Service (Hours)					

All four are women. Dillon pleaded guilty to "Disorderly" while the others pleaded guilty to "Parading." Both are Class B Misdemeanors, and both carry identical penalties so the difference in charge shouldn't account for the disparity in sentences. Only Friedman was a Democrat appointee, the rest were Republicans.

Dillon's attorney only cited 3 other women. In fact, there

were 11 women charged with "Parading." Of these 11 women, 3 got jail time (ranging from 14 to 60 days), 8 got probation (2 to 60 months), 3 got house arrest (30 to 60 days), and 9 got community service (40 to 120 hours). Looking only at those 6 women with no prior arrest records who came to D.C. without combat gear or disguises, 1 got jail time, 5 got probation (24 to 60 months), fines ranged from $0 to $5,000, 2 got house arrest (30 to 60 days) and all got community service (60 to 120 hours). So, the disparities are large whether or not the person had prior arrest records and came prepared for violence. Not only are the disparities large, but they are also consequential, often double (community service, house arrest) and occasionally even more (fines).

Screening for the next level, removing defendants with ties to extremist groups leaves 3 of the 6 women. For these 3 women, none got any jail time, and all got probation and community service. But only 1 got house arrest, and the ranges for the other elements were still wide for probation (24 to 60 months), fines ($0 to $5,000), and community service (60 to 120 hours). Bear in mind, the difference between $0 and $5,000 is not insubstantial, nor is the difference between 24 and 60 months.

In the prior analysis, the harshest sentence at every screening level belonged to a different Judge, from Walton (Bush) to Cooper (Obama) to Lamberth (Reagan): so Judges' proclivities are probably not at work. But all 3 women who got the harshest sentences were handled by DOJ supervising prosecutor Phillips.

Disparities in sentences like these were not uncommon. In a perfect world, differences in the defendants would account for the differences in sentences, but the system in which Jan 6 defendants are being handled is far from perfect. Consider the cases of Rachael Pert and Dana Winn – Both traveled from Florida with the intention to disrupt the voting. Both were Navy veterans and neither engaged in violence, theft, or property destruction during the 30+ minutes they were inside the Capitol. Both pleaded guilty to "Entering" though both had been charged with 4 other charges including "Aiding and Abetting". They faced a maximum of one year incarceration and $100,000 in fines. Pert had a prior arrest history including "disorderly conduct/battery on a law enforcement officer" and "driving while license suspended," but for some reason the DOJ did not comment on Winn. That omission is unusual because the DOJ often mentions that a defendant has no prior arrest records, so omitting any reference to Winn while referencing Pert is highly unusual and probably another example of inferior performance by the DOJ. FWIW – Pert/Winn was not the only example in which combined sentencing memorandum omitted details about one of the defendants (e.g., Harrison/Wangler).

In their recommendations the DOJ prosecutors admitted "Pert and Winn's conduct…are nearly identical," and recommended the same sentence for both - 3 months house arrest, 24 months' probation, 40 hours community service, and $500 restitution. But when it came time for ruling, Pert got twice as much time for probation - 24 months vs. 12 for Winn.

As illustrated, disparities without apparent reason were not uncommon. Most of the time, however, disparities could be accounted for by differences in the defendants. In four cases charged with "Disorderly," two people got jail time and two didn't. The two with jail time had prior arrest records but the other two did not. In two cases charged with "Threats," one person got twice as much jail time as the other. Though both had a history of drug problems, the one with ties to extremist groups and a history of violence got the lengthier sentence. In cases like these, the Justice system seems to be working, at least to the extent that people who deserved a harsher sentence got one. But did the sentence really fit the crime? Is 28 months in jail sufficient for a 53-year-old unemployed man who threatened to kill elected officials? Bear in mind he had ties to extremist groups and a history of violence, and he came to D.C. in combat gear and his social media comments indicated a desire to commit violence. As if his threats were not mere bravado, he was found in possession of an "assault-style rifle with a telescopic sight, a 9 mm semi-automatic firearm, over 2,500 rounds of ammunition, and multiple high-capacity magazines." Does a guy like this only get 28 months in jail?

Previously we looked at the statistics about the DOJ and the normal course of handling defendants. Here we'll compare what happened with the DOJ and the Jan 6 defendants compared to what usually happens.

Getting Caught

In 2020 the percent of criminals that got caught varied from 54% (murder) to 12% (motor vehicle theft). For crimes that had a violent component (e.g., assault, aggravated assault) the range was from 41% to 46%. Based on FBI estimates, in the nearly two years from the Jan 6 event, only 31% of the potential defendants were apprehended. The FBI most wanted list for Capitol defendants lists over 1,000 "items" of whom most are associated with "assault on federal officer." The list however only includes people for whom they have pictures. In summary, Jan 6 defendants appear to be nearly one-third less likely to be apprehended despite what the government has called the largest fugitive hunt in history.

Plea Agreements

More than 90% of misdemeanor cases brought by the federal government are settled through plea agreements. It's too early to decide what percent of the Jan 6 rioters will accept plea agreements. Plea agreements started in April 2021. Between April 2021 and November 2022 slightly more than 400 plea agreements were obtained. At this rate, with 900+ rioters, it will take more than 2 years to reach a 93% rate, which means it is unlikely that the Jan 6 rioters will achieve the "normal" plea agreement rate.

Release On Personal Recognizance

Most research at federal and state levels indicates that about two-thirds of defendants arrested for a misdemeanor get released on their own personal recognizance. For the 400+ Jan 6 misdemeanor defendants who agreed to pleas, upon arraignment, 71% were released on their own recognizance without any other conditions. The number increased to 90% with those who were required to put up a bond, and to 96% for those with some type of monitoring. Only 4% of the Jan 6 defendants arrested for a misdemeanor were put into pretrial detention.

Time

The average time from arrest to disposition for the average federal case for people who accept plea agreements is about 6 months. For the Jan 6 defendants, the average time was nearly a year. The range was 2.5 to 22 months. We are told that the Jan 6 case is the most intensive case the DOJ has ever handled, so the extra time to process defendants is understandable.

Sentences

In 2016 the median federal jail sentence for people convicted of misdemeanors was 6 months and the median probation time was 12 months. For Jan 6, the median jail sentence was 1.4 months, and the median probation time was 24 months.

MISDEMEANOR JAIL SENTENCES IN GENERAL AND FOR JAN 6 DEFENDANTS		
	Median Time	**Median Probation**
General	6 months	12 months
Jan 6	1.4 month	24 months

For violent felonies, 93% went to jail, 3% got probation only, 3% got a suspended sentence, and less than 1% got a fine only.

CONVICTIONS FOR VIOLENCE: GENERAL VS. JAN 6			
	Jail	**Probation**	**Suspended**
General	93%	3%	3%
Jan 6 (N=19)	100%	100%	0%

People convicted of disorderly conduct at the felony level went to jail 82% of the time, 12% probation only, and 6% suspended sentences.

CONVICTIONS FOR DISORDERLY: GENERAL VS. JAN 6			
	Jail	**Probation**	**Suspended**
General	82%	12%	12%
Jan 6 (N=10)	50%	80%	0%

Following Recommendations

In 2021 federal Judges followed DOJ recommendations/ guidelines in 68% of the cases, but Jan 6 Judges did so 11% of the time. Once the Judges strayed from the DOJ recommendations, Jan 6 Judges were far more inclined to rule in favor of the defendants by a ratio of more than 3:1. In both cases the defendant got the benefit of the Judge's rulings, but in general only 28% of judgments favored defendants while for Jan 6, the figure is 77%. Put another way, the chances for Jan 6 defendants to get a favorable ruling was nearly 3:1.

JUDGES FOLLOWING DOJ RECOMMENDATIONS			
	Neutral	Defendant	Prosecution
General	68%	28%	4%
Jan 6 (N=300)	11%	77%	12%

Probation

Probation allows the Justice system to keep track of a person's behavior when they are out of jail. Depending on the person's crime, the conditions of probation can vary widely. Probation can be given instead of a jail sentence, or it can be given in addition to a jail sentence. Federal guidelines recommend a period of supervised release following felony convictions. When deciding whether to impose a term of supervised release and for how long, federal judges must consider factors such as the recommendations in the federal sentencing guidelines, the nature of the current offense, the defendant's history, and the need to prevent the defendant from committing future crimes.

You would think that anyone whom a Judge would sentence to jail, given the demonstrated proclivity of Judges not to sentence Jan 6 defendants to jail, would demand that anyone sentenced to jail would also be sentenced to a period of supervised release to insure they do not engage in the same behavior in the future. When sentences are short, as they are in the case of the Jan 6 defendants, the need to follow-up is even more important. With a median jail sentence time of only 45 days, without supervised release, a defendant might re-engage with the people with whom they engaged with that led to the Jan 6 insurrection. Hence, the surprise that 37% of the Jan 6 misdemeanor defendants sentenced to jail are not sentenced to supervised release. The idea that nearly 40% of the Jan 6 defendants are being sentenced to jail but not to any probation term is just another example of the poor job the DOJ is doing. With a median term of only 45 days, many of these Jan 6 offenders will get back to doing what they were doing before the riot, and that bodes poorly for the future.

Given the seriousness of what these defendants did, it's vital that anyone deserving of probation (or supervised release) should have their behavior monitored to help ensure that they do not repeat. For this group of defendants, many of whom had prior arrest records, it's even more important to use probation as a time to help re-educate them, or at least, help modify their behavior. This action is not only in the best interests of the Nation, but also in the best interests of the defendants and their families.

Out of 300+ defendants who were sentenced as of November 2022, 85% received probation. Of these 256 people, only 53% received any special probation conditions. Of the 134 people with special conditions, the most used conditions were substance abuse testing (54), weapons restrictions (41), mental health treatment (37), substance abuse treatment (28), and mental health evaluation (20). Used less often were location restrictions (8), computer searching (5), social media restrictions (5), computer monitoring (5), education and vocational services (5), and curfews (1).

The chart shows the special conditions for misdemeanor and felony cases. Bear in mind the data is the number, not the percent, and bear in mind there are only 44 felony v 256 misdemeanor cases.

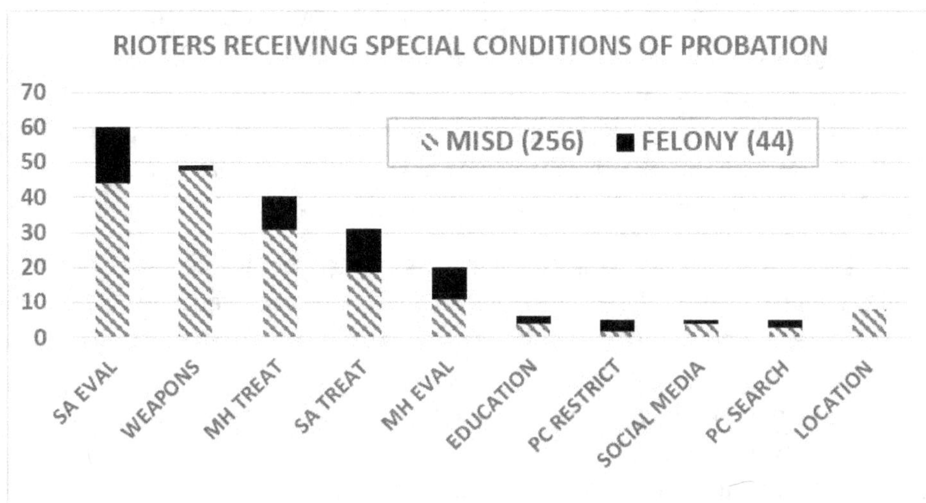

Note that felony defendants were significantly more likely to get substance abuse and mental health evaluation and treatment as well as PC and social media monitoring, however, they were less likely to get weapons restrictions.

Strangely, prior to June 2022, Judges gave weapons restrictions only 4 times. Since then they've used it dozens of times.

Matching the characteristics of the people sentenced with the special conditions attached to their sentences examines the appropriateness of the Judge's actions. People who have known mental health problems should get, at least, mental health evaluation. People known to have used social media to promote violence should have social media restrictions. People who used their computers to organize or conspire should have computer restrictions.

To determine whether or not a defendant had an associated problem (e.g., drug abuse, mental health, unemployed) or proclivity (e.g., using weapons, violent social media posts), the FBI reports, DOJ documents, and news media reports were examined. Then the special conditions were examined and then matching was performed. Ideally, there would be 100% agreement between the existence of an issue/proclivity and the special condition mandated as part of probation. In addition, there should be no false positives – people with no issue/proclivity being given a special condition that didn't apply to them (e.g., Why assign drug abuse treatment to someone who doesn't use drugs?).

This analysis looked at several issues/proclivities – substance abuse, mental health, unemployment, use of weapons, violent social media posts and use of computers to conspire to commit violence or illegal behaviors. Each of these issues/proclivities had a corresponding special probation condition(s). For example, someone with a drug abuse problem could be mandated for drug abuse assessment and drug abuse treatment.

Overall, the Judges did a poor job matching people and special conditions. Moreover, in most cases, they had an unacceptably high level of false positives and false negatives. It's hard to defend the poor performance of the Judges in this examination as they had all the information in front of them that I was able to obtain, and probably more. In addition, it's hard to come up with cases in which the Nation's well-being is in more peril than an attack on the Capitol, an occurrence which demands the best of our judicial system.

Some things to note from the 128 matching cases–

- By area, the overall correct matching was a mere 37%. False negatives exceeded correct matches (41% v 37%) while false positives were much less (19%).
- The highest correct scores were for Substance abuse (16%) and Mental health (14%), however, there were also substantial false positive errors (6% and 7% respectively) as well as false negatives (9% and 20%).
- The worst area was weapons – 10 people who used, brought with them, stored, or otherwise were involved in weapons were not identified by the Judges and given weapons restrictions. Two people who had no history of using weapons were both given weapons restrictions – "No Dangerous Weapons or Firearms- You must not

own, possess, or have access to a firearm, ammunition, destructive device, or dangerous weapon (i.e., anything that was designed, or was modified for, the specific purpose of causing bodily injury or death to another person such as nunchakus or tasers)."

- The most errors (35) happened in the area of mental health, and in this category the errors were higher in false negatives (26) rather than false positives (9). The largest single category of errors (12) was false negatives for Computer Use.
- Results for Drug Abuse and Employment were as good as flipping a coin – about 50% across the board. Computer use was slightly worse.

It's hard to say whether a false positive is worse than a false negative, though in a false positive, someone who doesn't need a service is required to get one. That's not a good use of government time/money and it's probably not doing much for a person's self-esteem. In a false negative, however, a person with a known problem isn't being given a service they might benefit from. Given the seriousness of this situation, failing to provide services to people in need seems to be criminal negligence at the least.

It's tempting to compare the error rate of the Judge's with their leniency scores and with the percent of the time they send defendants to jail. Both these measures have been discussed in previous research. Briefly, leniency is measured by comparing DOJ sentencing recommendations with Judge's rulings, yielding more lenient, more harsh, and neutral ratings. Leniency ranged from 100% to 6% with an average of 77% lenient, 19% harshly, and 11% neutral. Jail time is simply the percent that Judges gave jail to the defendants convicted of misdemeanors. Findings ranged from 100% to 0% with an average of 54%.

Leniency and jail time had a -0.67 correlation, meaning that Judges who were more lenient gave less jail time. That makes some sense. Both measures tap into a liberal tendency. The tendency was strongest among DEM-appointed Judges (-0.87) and less strong (though still directional) among GOP-appointees (-0.14).

Looking at the extent to which Judges made correct decisions when assigning special conditions of probation/supervised release, what can we say?

- Special conditions of probation were given in 53% of the cases in which probation was given. Judges missed an important opportunity to help influence the future behavior of the defendants.
- Judges used weapons restrictions, drug abuse and mental health conditions most often, but rarely used computer and social media restrictions. Given how many of the defendants used their computers to conspire, promote, and make threats of violence, ignoring the opportunity to exercise computer control is seriously negligent. There were over a dozen people for whom weapon use was a significant part of their background, including bringing or using weapons on Jan 6, and none of these people were restricted. This omission appears even worse than simple negligence.
- The overall score for correctly matching defendants' characteristics/behavior with available special conditions was a mere 37%. 37%! Whether this low score represents incompetence, indifference, poor presentation by the DOJ or over-worked Judges makes no difference – it is very troubling.
- False negatives (failing to give a person a condition they could benefit from, as in failing to offer substance abuse treatment to someone with a drug abuse problem) were more than twice as frequent as false positives (giving a condition to someone who didn't need it) – 41% vs 19%. The high number of false negatives is a future tragedy that might have been averted; now an opportunity lost.

The results of this research are deeply troubling. Judges are using special conditions of probation/supervised release about half the time. Given the nature of the defendants and their crimes, this is an important opportunity lost. The situation is even worse when you consider that social media restrictions are one of the least used conditions even while they are probably the most important issue to address. As if this isn't depressing enough, the error rate for weapons and social media restrictions are the highest.

Nearly a quarter of the Judges didn't get a single correct score, and the overall rate of correct matching was only 37%. A simple coin toss could do an equivalent job. It's difficult to explain this result. Are these Judges simply incompetent? Do they simply not care? Are they overworked? Did the DOJ fail to give them enough information to make correct decisions?

Having studied the DOJ and the Judges extensively, and probably more than any other person, my guess would be that the DOJ did fail to provide adequate information as well as appropriate recommendations. Having read more than 500 "Government Sentencing Memorandums" I recall less than a handful of recommendations about conditions of probation (e.g., Wagner, Riddle, Reimler, Ivey, Micajah). I also found that the information about the defendants was poorly presented. Hence, most of the blame attaches to the DOJ. But not all the blame.

There was enough material in the Defendant's Sentencing Memorandum and, in the trial, to alert perceptive and caring Judges to the problems of the defendants that warranted appropriate conditions of probation. Judge Chutkan got it right 100% of the time and 4 Judges got scores better than 50%, so there is no excuse for the rest of the mediocre performance by the dozen other Judges.

CHAPTER SUMMARY

The comparisons in this chapter are instructive, however, they are limited based on the sample size, the diversity of charges among the general population, and the demographic characteristics of the general population (e.g., Jan 6 defendants are almost exclusively White, general defendants are usually about one third White). With these limitations in mind, what can we say about the Jan 6 defendants that distinguishes them from the general population?

Here are the main points from this chapter –

- The character of the defendants bears on sentencing. More than 50% of the Jan 6 defendants sentenced had prior arrest records (e.g., child endangerment, drug possession, weapons possession, drug manufacturing, forcible entry) with 18% for assault (e.g., domestic violence, sexual battery). At least 39 had ties to extremist groups and at least 71 came to D.C. with combat gear or equipment, disguises, or posted on social media their intentions to commit violence, including shooting, hanging, stabbing, and spraying people.

- Only 54% got any jail time with a median sentence of 45 days. Only 28% received a fine (median $2,000), 85% received probation (median 24 months), 54% received community service (median 60 hours), and 28% received house arrest (median 60 days).

- Judges rejected DOJ recommendations for jail time in over a dozen cases and added jail time when not requested in only 5 cases. Jail time was more often given by Obama-appointed Judges than by Republican appointees, and Obama appointees were more likely to add probation.

- Defendants were looking at an average of 53 months in jail, but following DOJ recommendations, they faced only 8 months and after Judges ruled, they received only 6+ months.

- Compared to equivalent federal cases, J6 defendants were much more likely to be released on their own recognizance. Once sentenced, the J6 defendants averaged much less jail time (1.4 vs 6 months) but more probation time (24 vs. 12 months).

- Defendants got favorable treatment in 77% of the rulings while the Prosecution in only 12% and Judges followed the DOJ recommendations in only 11% of the cases. In equivalent federal cases, judges ruled in defendants' favor only 28% of the time.

- Judges did a poor job attaching special conditions of probation to the defendants that needed evaluation for mental health and drug abuse, educational and vocational services, and in restricting the use of weapons and social media where appropriate.

Overall, the Jan 6 defendants are treated better than the general federal defendants. This discrepancy flies in the face of AG Garland's remarks to Congress on October 21, 2021 when he said – "The rule of law is the foundation of our democracy. The essence of the rule of law is that like cases are treated alike." He went on to say – "…the Justice Department has undertaken an extraordinary effort to ensure that the perpetrators of criminal acts on January 6 are held accountable."

SENTENCES: JURY AND BENCH TRIALS

BENCH TRIALS

As of November 2022, 20 people submitted to Bench trials, beginning in March 2022, and averaging about 2 per month since. All but one was found guilty. The one who went free was courtesy of Trump-appointed Judge McFadden who openly expressed his concern about punishing rioters.

So far, only 5 of the 20 have been sentenced, even though their trials date back to June. Federal practice is usually 90 days between verdict and sentencing. By my calculations the average time, based on real and anticipated sentencing dates, is 120 days. Is the seemingly longer time between verdict and sentencing some form of punishment, overwork, or merely indifference?

FYI - The time between arrest and sentencing for bench trial rioters is 21 months compared to 19.5 months for jury trial rioters and 11 months for people who pleaded.

Verdicts for the 5 people have been on the light side, to say the least. Only one person (Griffin) was fined. Keep in mind that the true total costs of the Jan 6 riot exceed $30 million even though the DOJ only calculates some $2.5 million in direct costs. The current collection for all financial penalties (restitution, assessment, fines) based on 300+ people sentenced is a mere $1,320 per person. Should 1,000 people ever be found and charged (current number is 937), that's about half of what the DOJ's ridiculously low estimate accounts for.

Leniency is not limited to fines. Probation for 4 of the 5 is a mere 12 months, significantly less than the average for people who pleaded to identical crimes. Jail time for 2 of the 3 Misdemeanor cases is ZERO. That exceeds by a wide margin jail time for people who pleaded. And the one Misdemeanor case who got jail time, got a mere 14 days, also way below what pleading rioters got for identical offenses.

Two of the rioters at bench trials were guilty of more serious offenses. Rodean was found guilty of destruction (18 USC 1361) and 6 misdemeanors (one of which involved "physical violence" (18 USC 1752a4) in a restricted building). Hunter Seefried was found guilty of felony obstruction (18 USC 1512c22) and 4 misdemeanors.

Destruction, when it's under $100, is "punishable by a fine of up to $100,000, one year imprisonment, or both." Physical violence is punishable by "a fine under this title or imprisonment for not more than one year, or both..." Anyone found guilty of Obstruction "shall be fined under this title or imprisoned not more than 20 years, or both."

Hence, Rodean could have served 5 years in jail and been fined up to $100,000. Instead, he got no jail and no fine. Only one other person pleaded to destruction. He got 4 months for destruction alone. The 6 additional crimes for which Rodean was guilty got rioters who pleaded an average of slightly less than one year. All things considered, Rodean got off easier than those who pleaded

Seefried, for obstruction, could have served 5 years in jail and been fined up to $100,000. Instead, he got 2 years in jail and no fine. Six rioters who pleaded guilty to obstruction <u>alone</u> got an average of 2.4 years' jail (range 8 to 55 months) and no fine. That's when obstruction alone is considered, but Seefried had obstruction plus 4 misdemeanors. The average sentence for people with similar misdemeanors (without a felony) was slightly less than one year. All things considered, Seefried got off easier than those who pleaded.

It's worthy nothing that both Nordean and Seefried were tried before Trump-appointed Judge McFadden, the same judge responsible for letting Matthew Martin go free.

In summary, rioters who opt for Bench Trials wait about 4 months from trial to sentencing but they are being rewarded with substantially more lenient jail sentences than rioters charged with identical offenses who pleaded. Given that those who pleaded are already getting more lenient treatment, this additional level of leniency is questionable. However, it must be noted that the subject pool is small and one of the most pro-rioter Judges has been used disproportionately more often.

JURY TRIALS

As of November 2022, 19 people submitted to a jury trial and 7 were sentenced. All but 1 (Larson-Olson) were charged with multiple felonies and all were found guilty. In almost all cases it took the juries less than 5 hours to come to a verdict, and all defendants were convicted on almost all the charges.

For the 6 charged with a felony, the most common charges were Obstruction (5), Civil Disorder (3), Possession of a Deadly Weapon (2), and Assault with a Deadly Weapon (1). Other charges included theft, violent entry, entering, disorderly, and parading. Average liability for the felony-charged defendants was more than 25 years. They were all White males.

Only 1 of the 5 rioters (Webster) was not found guilty of Obstruction. Comparing the 5 people found guilty of Obstruction who pleaded vs. the 6 who went to a jury with the same charge, the average jail time was 4.5 years (Jury) vs. 2.4 years (Pleaded). The percent fined was similar – 40% (Jury) vs. 0% (Pleaded).

It appears that rioters have better outcomes with a plea than a jury trial. So why would riots elect a jury trial? As my previous research demonstrated, rioters with ties to extremists are less likely to elect pleas because of their cult-like loyalty to the cause and the psychological problems of cognitive dissonance, an issue I've dealt with at length previously.

Of course, the small samples here require that the data be looked at with some skepticism until more data comes in. That being said, it is illuminating.

SUMMARY OF BENCH AND JURY TRIALS

As of November 22, about 10% of those rioters who were tried opted for a bench or jury trial, and of those, only a dozen were sentenced. Rioters who chose either one of these options were almost exclusively felony cases and had a high proportion of people with ties to extremist groups. They were White males with only a few exceptions. Generally speaking, sentences were harsher than for people who pleaded, and it took longer for them to get a sentence.

SENTENCES: WOMEN AND NON-WHITES

The previous chapters dealt with sentencing in general. Because previous research indicates that women and non-Whites are treated differently than the White male rioters, this chapter will focus on those two groups.

WOMEN RIOTERS

In my book "Insurrection: The Riot," among many other things, I developed a profile for the women rioters and compared that with women in general and against the male non-violent and the male violent rioters. As of November 2022 women were 15% of the 900+ charged.

At the time of first writing this book few women had been sentenced. By May 2022 there were 30 women who pleaded guilty and were sentenced, and by November there were 55 women in the subject pool.

While women were 15% of those arrested, they were 18% of those with plea agreements who've been sentenced and 19% of the those with plea agreements awaiting sentencing. The women sentenced differ somewhat from the total women arrested on about half the 100 variables I studied. Those who pleaded came from smaller cities (28,149 v 34,073) were younger (39 v 50), less White (82% v 100%), less likely to be professionals (4% v 18%) and business owners or managers (22% v 27%), more likely to have financial problems (54% v 48%), more likely to have clean police records (40% v 20%) and less likely to have ties with extremist groups (28% v 32%). They were equally likely to be married and have children, be overweight, blond, Republican, and to have come to D.C. with a spouse. None of the women who pleaded were charged with violence while 9 of the 135 women arrested were. The bottom line is that the women who pleaded are not a representative sample of the total women arrested.

To do an analysis of whether the women rioters were treated differently than the male rioters, it was necessary to eliminate all the males guilty of felonies, reducing the male subject pool. There were several issues that interested me. Did women equally get the same percent of sentences or the same average sentence length? Were Judges equally lenient with men and women? Did Judges give special conditions of probation equally to men and women, and in equal proportions?

Bear in mind, the charges are all misdemeanors, and many of the women who pleaded were part of a husband/wife or boyfriend/girlfriend team (e.g., Bustle, Miller, Pert, Pettit, Schubert, Wilson, Vinson) both of whom were sentenced. There were also male/female relatives (e.g., Hernandez/Merry) and male/female friends (e.g., Fitchett/Sweet, Cudd/Rosa, Kelley/Quick) arrested and sentenced. Hence, more than half the women sentenced were sentenced along with a male whom they were closely matched with.

Sentencing

To begin we'll look at the percent of time Judges assign women v men to the five major sentencing options (jail, probation, fine, community service, house arrest). The data is presented in the chart.

Most of the figures are relatively close except for house arrest, where men far exceed women (36% v 20%). Men also exceeded women in being sent to jail more often (49% v 43%) while women exceeded men in getting probation (89% v 82%) and community service (67% v 57%), though these differences were minor. Being fined was nearly identical (31% v 34%). All things considered it appears that men are treated more harshly, but not to any great degree.

In addition to the percent of time Judges assigned defendants to sentencing elements, we can see if the amount of time or the amount of the penalty differed. Women got less jail time (30 v 41 days) but more probation (36 v 24 months) and higher fines ($2,000 v $1,500). House arrest (60 days) and Community service (60 hours) were identical.

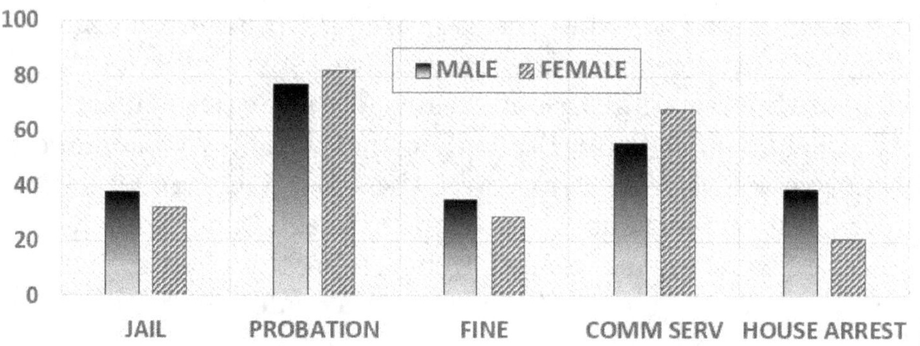

Conditions Of Probation

Judges can assign a defendant to extra experiences during their probation. Ideally, the experiences match their needs; hence, a known substance abuser might be given substance abuse testing or treatment, or a known social media junkie who advocated violence might be given social media restrictions, or someone with mental health problems might be required to have a mental health evaluation. There are more than a dozen possibilities Judges used, though generally speaking, Judges for Jan 6 only used them about half the time.

Females compared to males got a special condition about as often (46% v 50%), but they differed substantially in what special conditions were assigned. Women most often were assigned mental health treatment (22%) while for men the most frequent condition was substance abuse testing (22%). Nearly 30% of all special conditions assigned to women dealt with mental health evaluation or treatment while for men it was 20%. These results imply that either the women have significantly more mental health issues or the Judges look upon the behavior of the women as reflecting mental health.

To test this hypothesis, I compared the mental health indicators (e.g., ADD, AHDD, drug addiction, alcoholism, traumatic brain injury, psychiatric hospitalization) for the men and the women. Females and males were almost even though women were slightly less involved (22% v 26%). Hence, while the female defendants presented with slightly less mental health challenges, Judges nonetheless required mental health procedures for a greater percentage of women (22% v 15%). This appears to suggest a bias by the Judges against women, possibly reflecting a Judge's idea that "A woman would have to be crazy to do a thing like this!"

With substance abuse, 15% of women got substance abuse testing and 10% got treatment. Among men it was 22% and 10%, suggesting that men were more likely to be presenting with substance abuse problems. Using the percent of defendants arrested for DUI or other alcohol problems or drug abuse, 20% of the women and 34% of the men showed up. So, the greater frequency for referring men for testing appears appropriate.

To summarize, while men and women are getting about the same percent of special conditions of probation, and while they have about the same degree of mental health problems, the women get more mental health conditions assigned even while having fewer mental health conditions. Regarding substance abuse evaluation, the assignment of conditions appears appropriate.

But what sentence the Judges gave is only half the story. The other half of the story is how often they got it right. I randomly chose 6 men and women from 6 different Judges and looked at the correct matching for what they ordered and the defendant's characteristics. Judges don't always get it right and these Judges in this case rarely got it right. Looking only at substance abuse and mental health, Judges correctly assigned conditions for 40% of the men and only 17% of the women.

Here are some examples of (what I consider) poor matching of conditions of probation with the defendant's characteristics –

- According to the FBI and DOJ reports, Nicole Prado had a history of DUI, but Obama-appointee Judge Contreras didn't think to offer substance abuse evaluation. Instead, he placed her on a 2-month, 7pm curfew with no apparent reason for the curfew and without the DOJ's recommendation.
- According to the FBI and DOJ reports, Rachel Pert had a history of battery including battery against law enforcement and resisting law enforcement among other offences. She showed up with a flagpole intending to use it as a weapon in D.C. Despite these signs, Trump-appointee Judge McFadden didn't see fit to require anger management or mental health evaluation.
- According to the FBI and DOJ reports, Gracyn Courtright was a student at the University of Kentucky, living with her parents. She was found carrying a "Members Only" sign and returned it to an Officer: otherwise, she committed no violence, nor destruction, nor advocated violence on social media. Obama appointed Judge Cooper assigned her for mental health evaluation.
- According to the FBI and DOJ reports, Traci Sundstrum came to D.C. wearing a ridiculous outfit that defies brief description. She wore a hat with Q printed on the front.

She used foul language and exhorted the rioters for further action. She posted that Antifa was at the riot. Despite these indications, Judge Cooper saw no reason to request mental health evaluation.

- According to the FBI and DOJ reports, Virginia Spencer had a history of drug and paraphernalia possession. The DOJ noted - "The defendant has struggled with narcotics addiction in the past..." but Clinton-appointee Judge Kollar-Kotelly didn't think to ask for substance abuse evaluation.

When you lay out the information in this manner it's truly hard to understand why these Judges did what they did? Incompetence? Lack of concern? Too busy schedule?

Leniency

Leniency is defined as the extent to which Judges differed from recommendations made by the DOJ, giving defendants less than the DOJ recommended. Keep in mind that the DOJ already gave Jan 6 defendants unprecedented leniency, reducing an average of 4+ charges to a single charge, throwing out felonies for dozens of people, refusing to charge dozens of people with lying to the FBI and/or destroying evidence. Further leniency on top of what was already handed out would seem to be a slap in the Nation's face, but it's what happened anyway.

Overall, Judges gave more lenient sentences in 77% of the cases. Removing the felony cases and comparing the 55 female v 201 male defendants charged with misdemeanors, Judges gave even more leniency to 81% of the men and 77% of the women. These differences are small and insignificant.

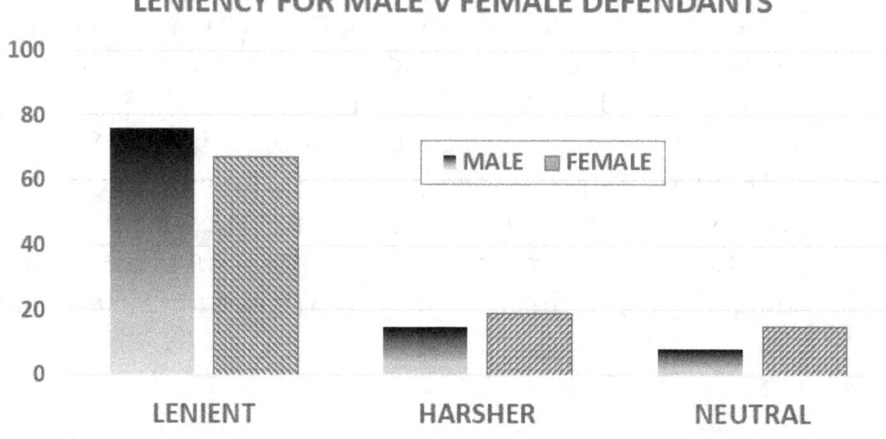

Summary Of Women Rioters

In this section we compared 55 women and 201 men sentenced for misdemeanors as of November 2022.

-    While women and men had similar known problems with mental health, the women were getting significantly more mental health referrals. Do Judges think women have to be crazier than men to be involved in the Jan 6 riot? Or do these Judges simply think women are less stable (without any evidence to back them up)?

-    In correctly matching defendant's needs/characteristics with the conditions of probation, Judges got it right in 40% of the cases for males and only 17% for females. Are Judges paying less attention to the needs of the women? Or do they simply not care enough to spend time trying to pick a good condition for the women?

-    The percent of time Judges gave out sentencing elements differed significantly, with men getting jail and house arrest more often, while women got probation and community service more often. All things considered, women got the better deal.

-       In the severity of the sentences, median house arrest and community service were identical, but women got less jail time though more probation and higher fines. Strangely enough, women were required to complete their community service in twice the time required of men, another outcome favoring women.

-       Comparing Judges' rulings with DOJ recommendations, there were no significant differences in leniency toward men or women.

In theory there should be no differential treatment for men v women in the Justice system even though in the broader society women do get traditional deferrals ("women and children first"). Nonetheless, there were a great many differences between how men and women who pleaded guilty to misdemeanors for their behavior on January 6 were treated. In a few cases treatment seemed to be equal, but in the overwhelming number of comparisons there were differences favoring women.

It's difficult to say, on an overall basis, whether men or women are the "winners" in these comparisons. What is shocking is that there are so many differences in a system that is supposed to be dispensing Justice equally.

NON-WHITES

Among the 900+ people arrested for participating in the Jan 6 insurrection, almost all were White, but there were a small number of non-Whites, mostly Hispanics, and as of November 2022, 36 agreed to pleas, 22 were sentenced, and 48 maintained their innocence. Given the differences we found between males and females, it's worthwhile to look at the differences between Whites and non-Whites, bearing in mind the relatively low subject pool of non-Whites.

Background

Of the 400+ people who pleaded, the overall plea rate for non-Whites was 35% compared to an overall 42% for Whites. The lower overall plea rate for non-Whites was due to the low plea rate for male non-Whites (30%) compared to female non-Whites (63%). Among male non-whites, the highest plea rates were Blacks (53%), Asians (43%), Hispanics (24%) and Others (0%).

About 10% of the people sentenced were non-White (16 Hispanic, 4 Black, 1 Asian, 1 Middle-Easterner). Women were 27%. Comparing the demographics of the two groups, Whites came from smaller towns (23,478 v 97,279), had more blue-collar workers (37% v 20%), and were less likely to have prior arrests (53% v 71%), to have a BA or higher (35% v 42%), and belong to extremist groups (24% v 33%). They were similar in median age and percent holding professional positions.

Of the 22 non-Whites sentenced, all but 4 pleaded to a misdemeanor, mostly Parading. It's difficult to make judgments when the subject pool is only 4 non-whites.

Turning to the non-whites who pleaded to misdemeanors, almost all were males. They had a median age of 33 years and lived in cities with a median size of 70,000. Compared to the Whites who were sentenced, non-Whites were younger, from larger cities, more educated, and less likely to have a military or Police background. They were equally likely to have ties to extremist groups (about 23%) and to have "clean" prior arrest records (35%), though their prior arrest records were much less likely to include assault.

Violence

Because violent behavior can determine sentencing, it's important to look at whether or not non-Whites were more or less violent. The first graph shows violent intentions by race. Non-whites exceeded Whites on all 3 measures, through the differences were relatively small and not statistically significant. However, the small differences in each element added up to substantial overall differences (57% v 45%).

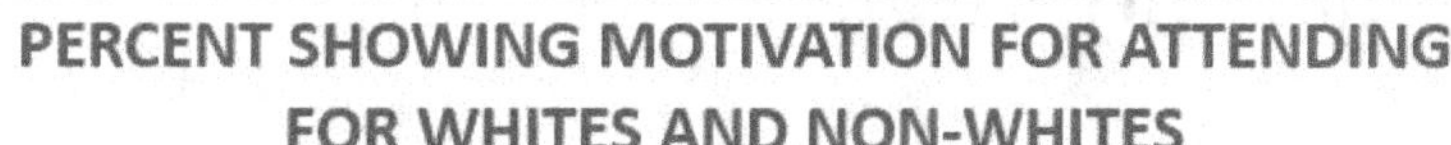
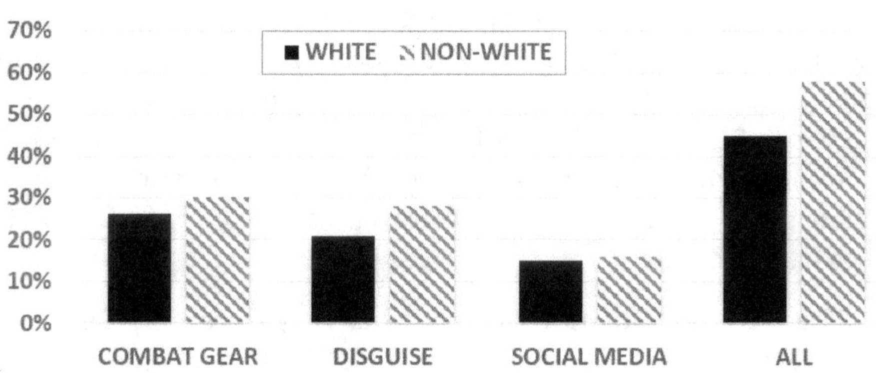

Violent behavioral intentions did not translate into verbal claims of motivation for non-Whites. Only 8% of non-Whites indicated that their reason for attending the D.C. event was violence. This contrasts with the 16% of Whites who mentioned violence as a reason to go to D.C. Both groups indicated that protesting the election was their main reason.

Though non-Whites had significantly higher violent intentions and significantly lower expressed motivations to engage in violence, about 20% of Whites and non-Whites were both charged with violent acts (mostly assault). One interesting note is that (as of November 2022) among non-Whites who pleaded, only 6% were charged with violence while among those who did not plead, 39% were charged with violence.

Given that non-Whites were charged with about the same percent of violence, we should expect that this important variable is not at play when ultimately looking at sentencing. However, it's important to note that among those who pleaded and were sentenced, violence by non-Whites was much lower than for Whites.

Community Service

The first difference that attracted my attention was the use of community service. More than half the White defendants received community service with an average of 80 hours and a range from 20 to 250. When Judges gave a time frame in which to complete the community service, the White defendants got a median of 18 months. In very rare cases, the Judges forgot to assign a time frame.

The situation for non-Whites was very different. Only one third got community service, and none of them were given a time frame.

What's going on?

Only 1 of the 8 judges who sentenced the non-White defendants was also non-White. Curiously, he assigned Alvear-Gonzales to 200 hours of community service. The other 7 White Judges used community service only twice. Do White Judges have a problem assigning non-White defendants to community service?

Given our finding that violence was substantially less for non-Whites sentenced, less community services makes no sense.

Leniency

The next element to examine was leniency, and among lenient rulings, jail time is the most important element. Whites got more lenient sentences 80% of the time compared to Non-Whites at 94%. This is one of the few elements in which non-Whites did better, however, this data (leniency) is a relative figure. It's determined by the difference between DOJ recommendations and Judges' rulings. Thus, if the DOJ discriminates against non-Whites in their recommendations and the Judges' rule more leniently, it may reflect the DOJ's discrimination rather than leniency per se.

To determine what's going on here, I compared the DOJ recommendations for non-Whites vs Whites. To further examine the data, I eliminated all felons and compared 136 White defendants v 18 non-Whites. Non-Whites got DOJ recommendations for jail time 73% of the time, while Whites were 75%. Non-Whites got DOJ recommendations for an average of 42 days jail time, while Whites got 48 days.

It's hard to explain these results, especially since the subject pool of non-Whites for this part of the study is only 18 people. The recommendations do not differ substantially but when push-comes-to-shove, there is a big difference in Judges' leniency.

In the end, the average percent of people receiving jail time was 47% for Whites and 41% for non-Whites. The average sentence length was 48 days for Whites and 45 days for non-Whites. So, the final differences were minimal, even as they were in the DOJ recommendations.

Summary Of Non-White Rioters

Here's what we found-

- It took the DOJ slightly longer to process non-Whites compared to Whites (337 v 321 days).
- Based on DOJ reports, Whites and non-Whites got recommendations for jail time about as often (75% v 73%) and the median jail sentence recommended length was also similar (48 days v 42 days).
- Based on actual rulings, Whites and non-Whites got jail time about as often (47% v 41%) and the median jail sentence recommended length was also similar (48 days v 45 days).
- Judges gave special conditions of probation to Whites and non-Whites at the same level overall, but non-Whites got significantly more referrals for substance abuse evaluation/treatment.
- Judges correctly matched defendants needs with special conditions of probation at a higher level for Whites than non-Whites (55% v 37%), and the incidence of false negatives (not giving someone what they needed) was much lower for non-Whites (17% v 41%), while false positives (giving someone something they didn't need) was much higher (17% v 4%). Non-White Judges did not perform differently than White Judges
- Non-Whites got significantly less community service, whether we looked at the percent of time they got community service, the average amount of time they got, and the time limit in which they were required to complete the service.

Analysis of these results should take into account the small number of non-Whites in the study. Where possible, median scores were used to adjust for the low number of subjects, however, it's still difficult to generalize. That being said, since more than 90% of the rioters were White, the total number of non-Whites will always be much smaller, regardless of the comparisons.

CHAPTER SUMMARY

This chapter looked at sentencing for non-Whites and women. In both cases there were substantial differences between the treatment of White males and the two groups. One of the biggest differences was the assignment of special conditions of probation, with both groups getting differential treatment and Judges performing correct matching less often.

On the other hand, neither group took significantly longer to process, each taking slightly less than a year.

Judges were more lenient toward non-Whites but there were no differences for men v women. Women got jail time less often and less time to serve, though more probation and longer sentences. For non-Whites there were no differences. In an ideal world, there would be no differences. All things considered, the differences here are not substantial even while they do exist.

BLM V JAN 6

It's hard to evaluate the sentencing for Jan 6 participants without some perspective. Do Judges uniformly ignore DOJ recommendations and opt to rule in favor of defendants? If they do, then there is nothing unusual going on with the Jan 6 defendants. On the other hand, if the leniency shown to Jan 6 participants is unusual, then something is going on. We already looked at the differences between Jan 6 and normal federal defendants. To do a further comparative analysis I chose the BLM protests with an emphasis on peaceful BLM protests.

Unfortunately, there isn't much research on the BLM protesters, though there are lots of anecdotal reports and cases studies. Moreover, BLM protests are diverse, not merely over time but over place and some involve riots and violence, and some do not. Here is what I've been able to find.

GENERAL

During most BLM protests hundreds of protesters have been arrested on the spot. At the Capitol "protest," only a handful of people were similarly arrested. One study in Portland Oregon found that because of the aggressive arrest policy used against BLM protesters, 90% of the charges had to be dropped. In the Capitol cases, arrests have been delayed and slow, hence, less than 1% were dropped. Nearly two years after the fact, only about 30% were even charged while most BLM protesters were charged by the next day.

BLM protesters got the attention of the U.S. President. In June 2020, he threatened them with "lengthy prison sentences" and in July he tweeted a "minimum 10 years in prison." Capitol protesters, on the other hand, were told by the same President that he loved them and asked them to go home. They weren't threatened with anything.

At the BLM protest in June 2020, the National Guard, armed and wearing camouflage uniforms, met the protesters and quickly dispersed caustic spray. On Jan 6, the National Guard was only activated after the rioters were inside the Capitol. 88 BLM protesters were detained on the spot. On Jan 6 it was less than a dozen.

An analysis of 7,750 demonstrations in 2,400 locations found 93% happened with no violence. On Jan 6, over 200 of the 900+ people arrested were charged with violence.

In 2020, more than 14,000 people were arrested for BLM protests. An analysis found that most of the protesters had no prior arrest records and no ties to Antifa or other extremist groups. Of the 900+ people arrested for Jan 6, more than half had prior arrest records and 30% had ties to an extremist group.

Over a period of 5 months in 2020, 950 cases of Police brutality against civilians and journalists were reported at BLM protests. Not a single case of Police brutality was brought on Jan 6. The one case in which a rioter was shot by Police was judged to be appropriate given the circumstances.

The AP reported that in 2021 70 BLM defendants who pleaded to federal crimes like arson and conspiracy got an average of 27 months in jail and "at least 10" got 5 or more years in jail. Of the 300+ Jan 6 defendants who pleaded guilty, almost half got no jail time, and only 1 person got 5 or more years in jail. Several were charged with conspiracy, obstruction, assault, theft, weapons possession, and destroying property, but the DOJ dropped almost all these major felonies in favor of misdemeanors.

An analysis of federal policy for pretrial detention found that starting in 2018 this practice increased and federal prosecutors "are now more likely to request detention for federal defendants than at any time since at least 2006." More than 20% of the BLM protesters were being detained. According to my database, less than 5% of the Jan 6 defendants were being detained prior to trial while more than 60% were released on their personal recognizance with no bond, no ankle bracelets, and no conditions whatsoever.

CASE STUDIES

These general examples show a pattern. Here are some individual case studies of sentences for BLM protesters whose crimes are similar to Jan 6 rioters.

Shamar Betts, a recent high school graduate with no prior criminal record, was charged with inciting a riot via Facebook, and detained prior to his trial. He was given 4 years in prison (Prosecutors had asked for the maximum 5 years prison sentence) and ordered to pay $1.5 million in restitution (Prosecutors recommended $2 million). To pay this, the court ordered that after release, all his disposable income every month to be seized.

FWIW – In Capital riot cases, DOJ prosecutors almost never asked for maximum sentences. Jan 6 rioters who contributed to $30,000,000 in damages were normally asked for a mere $500 restitution payment. Dozens of rioters incited the Capitol riot on FB and not even one was so-charged, though two people were charged with "Interstate threats" that were more targeted. Finally, very few Capitol rioters were kept in jail prior to trial.

Emmanuel Quinones a 25-year-old who brought an assault rifle to a Texas BLM demonstration (where open-carry is lawful) after he posted on FB that he would "off racists and MABA people," was sentenced to 46 months in prison. In contrast, dozens of Capitol rioters used social media to claim they would attack, knife, shoot, and hang people on Jan 6. A handful also showed up with weapons. None were charged with using social media to threaten general violence and an exceedingly small number were charged with weapons possession. None have been sentenced to date.

Two BLM protestors in Brooklyn who destroyed a Police car were labeled "terrorists" and charged with crimes carrying a 45-year mandatory minimum sentence. Not a single rioter, even the dozens who used weapons against Police face a 45-year sentence, and none were labeled terrorists.

In Richmond Virginia 13 demonstrators who blocked traffic on I-95 were sentenced to 5 days in jail. In contrast, nearly half of the rioters who illegally trespassed onto the Capitol grounds, intent on disrupting Congress from lawfully fulfilling its constitutional obligations, got no jail time at all.

24-year-old Elias Bautista was a leader in a BLM protest in San Luis Obispo in 2021. Police charged him with one felony and two misdemeanor counts, and in the plea agreement offered to drop the misdemeanors and proceed with the felony, giving Bautista 60 days in jail and 2 years of probation.

Matthew Bruce, a 25-year-old leader in a BLM protest in Iowa in 2020 pleaded guilty to the only felony and in return they dropped 6 other charges. He's looking at 10 years jail and a $13,000 fine. Meanwhile, since his original arrest he's been arrested 4 more times for protest-related activities. Bruce had no criminal record prior to these arrests.

FWIW – the normal plea agreement in an analogous situation with Jan 6 rioters is to remove the felony and an average of 3 misdemeanors, and only proceed with the misdemeanor, for which nearly half the people got no jail time at all. Notice that in these cases the BLM "leaders" are prosecuted. Also note that these are younger-aged people with no arrest records. A third of Jan 6 protesters had prior arrest records and were on average about 40 year-old. No Jan 6 "leaders" have yet been charged or arrested.

In 2020 El Paso County, Colorado authorities refused to offer plea agreements to more than a dozen BLM protesters who allegedly blocked traffic on I-25. As far as I know, the DOJ is not "refusing" to offer plea agreements to anyone. Plea agreements have been made with several violent offenders and nearly a dozen members of extremist groups. DOJ plea agreements were made with child abusers, rapists, people convicted of attempted murder, and other upstanding citizens. But the dangerous obstruction of a highway is so serious no plea agreements can be made!

From a different perspective, a couple in Missouri were convicted of waving guns at BLM protesters and subsequently pardoned by the Republican Governor.

SUMMARY FOR BLM

These individual cases show a pattern, just as the general issues showed a pattern. It's clear that BLM protesters were treated very differently from the Jan 6 protesters, and more specifically, BLM protesters were treated more harshly. Here's a summary of what the data suggests. I've tried to put them in some type of chronological order –

- BLM protesters were more likely to be labeled "terrorists" or "insurrectionists" by Government officials.
- BLM protests were usually met quickly with heavily armed Police and/or National Guard presence. The Jan 6 protesters were met with Police who were not armed for violence and the National Guard presence was delayed for hours.
- Police were more likely to brutalize BLM protesters while Jan 6 protesters were more likely to brutalize Police.
- Less than 10% of BLM protests involved violence while nearly 25% of Jan 6 protesters were arrested for violence.
- Due to aggressive arrest policies, most people arrested at BLM protests were released without charges or charges were dropped. For Jan 6 protesters, fewer than 1% of the people arrested had their charges dropped.
- BLM protesters were more than twice as likely to be detained prior to trial.

- BLM protesters were less likely to be offered plea agreements.
- BLM protesters were less likely to have felony charges dismissed.
- BLM protesters were more likely to face longer jail terms for the same offenses, even while BLM protesters were less likely to have prior arrest records.
- Aggressive efforts were made to find and prosecute BLM "leaders". Similar efforts have not been made with the people who planned the Jan 6 event.

Hence, not only does it "appear" that the Jan 6 protesters were being treated leniently, when compared to BLM protesters it's noticeably clear that in every respect, Jan 6 protesters were treated more leniently. The caveat here is that no one has studied the BLM protests to the extent that I studied the Jan 6 protest, and therefore the conclusions are, to some extent, tentative even while compelling.

WHO PAYS THE COSTS OF JAN 6?

We do!

Among the far too many questions raised by the performance of the DOJ in managing the Jan 6 prosecutions is their claim that the costs of the riot were $1.5 million dollars and their practice of charging the defendants a "restitution" fee of $500 for misdemeanors and $2,000 for felonies. Generally speaking, people ultimately charged with felonies accounted for only 10% of those sentenced, even though upon arrest felony charges were 25% of the total. The reason for the decrease is the DOJ propensity to drop felonies in favor of misdemeanors.

By November 2022 the number of new people being charged/arrested dwindled to 1 or 2 per week. It's safe to say that when all is said and done, the DOJ will charge about 1,000 people of whom 900 will be misdemeanors and 100 felonies. Do the math – 900 misdemeanor cases charged $500 apiece equals $450,000 in restitution. Add 100 felony cases charged $2,000 apiece equals $200,000. Hence, the DOJ will recover $650,000 of the $1.5 million. Only if by some miracle, the FBI arrests all 3,000 people believed to have been involved, the return would be $1,950,000. The chances of this happening are nearly zero.

This example of poor math didn't escape the watch of the news media, nor did it escape the scrutiny of Judges. In August 2021, Chief Judge Beryl Howell when sentencing 46-year-old Wes Croy who agreed to pay $500 in restitution said -"I'm accustomed to the government being fairly aggressive in seeking restitution. Where we have Congress appropriating all this money due directly to the events on January 6, I have found the damage amount of less than $1.5 million, when all of us American taxpayers are about to foot the bill for close to half a billion dollars, a little bit surprising," she said.

"The cost of repairing damages from the attack on the U.S. Capitol and related security expenses have already topped $30 million and will keep rising", said the Architect of the Capitol J. Brett Blanton in February 2021. Blanton said that the Congressional Appropriations Committee had already approved a transfer request of $30 million to pay for expenses and extend a temporary perimeter fencing contract through March 31, 2021.

The Justice Department first disclosed the $1.5 million figure in a May 27, 2021, letter to the defense lawyer for Paul Hodgkins, a Florida man who pleaded guilty to one count of obstructing an official proceeding. They wrote - "Your client acknowledges that the riot that occurred on January 6, 2021, caused as of May 17, 2021, approximately $1,495,326.55 damage to the United States Capitol."

As far as I can tell, the first time costs are specifically mentioned for sentencing purposes is the November 9, 2021 DOJ Government Sentencing Memorandum for Jacob Chansley in which the DOJ writes on page 4 – "The substantial damage to the U.S. Capitol required the expenditure of nearly $1.5 million dollars for repairs." They base this number of several documents including a Feb 24, 2021 statement by Farar Elliott, the Curator of the House. In that document Elliott focuses on several statues and busts (Jefferson, Adams, Madison). Elliott requested "a supplemental appropriation of $25,000 for support of emergency repair and conservation of the House Collection objects."

The other document is a May 19, 2021 statement from J. Brett Blanton, Architect of the Capitol in which he describes government efforts to assess the damages. He notes on page 3 that "The Appropriations Committees approved a transfer request of $30,000,000 that addressed the AOC's initial expenses incurred, including funding for the temporary perimeter fencing requested by the USCP."

How the DOJ came up with a $1.5 million estimate based on the $25,000 or the $30,000,000 figures is a good question. When asked by news media to explain this number, the DOJ refused to comment. This issue is simply one of many issues that raises the question of what's happening in the DOJ.

Apparently concerned with the question of costs, the DOJ revised the cost estimates from $1.5 to $2.73 million in April 2022 during a hearing for Anthony Vuksanaj. But these cost estimates failed to take into account the payroll costs for Police, the equipment and supplies used/destroyed, the payroll for FBI investigations, DOJ prosecution, jail time for the 10% who were detained, etc.

Using the revised DOJ estimate of $2.73 million, their maximum, beyond hope, restitution would generate $1.9 million, leaving the taxpayers to shell out nearly $1 million. But the $2.73 million figure is so ridiculously low, as noted above, the true costs to taxpayers is more likely to be multiple millions of dollars.

Putting aside the poor math, how much is the DOJ collecting? As of November 2022, the DOJ collected a total of $395,108 from 300 defendants. The total includes restitution, fines, and assessment fees. That's an average of $1,321 per person. Moving forward, for 1,000 people sentenced, the total collected would be $1.3 million, leaving the taxpayer to come up with the deficit, which exceeds $30 million.

FRUIT OF THE POISON TREE

I saved this chapter for near the end because in some ways it's the most important chapter of all. This chapter was written originally as a study and sent to the DOJ in January 2022. It is reproduced here exactly as it was sent then. Following this report there is an up-to-date analysis of the DOJ website.

METHODOLOGY

Materials

The un-titled DOJ internal document (variously referred to as "Exhibit Table of Sentences", "Table of Sentences in Capitol Breach Cases", "Exhibit Sentencing Chart," etc.) contains information including defendant's name, case number, offense, government recommendation, and sentence imposed. It is used for the purposes of avoiding sentence disparity. Hereafter referred to as UD.

In order for the judicial process to work, the information in this document needs to be accurate. If this information is not accurate, recommendations based on this document cannot be valid. If the recommendations made, based wholly or partially on this document, and used by the DOJ and/or the Judges, are based on inaccurate information, then the sentences themselves must be questioned if sentence disparity is to be avoided.

The latest version of this document is 01/20/22. It contains the same information as in previous versions, with new additions.

Method

I examined in detail the UD which listed eighty-two cases, which was 87% of the total people sentenced as of January 31, 2022. I examined the original Government Sentencing Memorandum (GSM) and the Judge's Ruling (JR) and compared that information to the information in the UD.

There is minimal annotation. The tables are divided into three categories – probation without home detention (6 cases), probation with home detention (27 cases), and incarceration (49 cases).

Not every comparison could be made because DOJ documents are not easily available, despite Freedom of Information requests. In any event, seventy-six comparisons were capable of being made.

Errors were categorized as minor or major.

Minor Errors

An example of a minor error would be forgetting to mention location monitoring as part of home detention or forgetting to mention drug testing, mental health treatment, employment, or similar factors when mentioning probation. Another series of minor errors documented were the omission of the "assessment" or the "special assessment" charged to most, but not all the defendants.

A word needs to be said about the issue of "assessment." Often the DOJ refers to "mandatory assessment," but the amount of the assessment varies, from $10 to as much as $200 (e.g., Fairlamb) and while $10 is the most common assessment, $100 is not unusual (e.g., Hodgkins, Smocks, Chansley, Meredith, Thompson, Palmer, etc.). Sometimes the assessment is mentioned (e.g., Sweet, Brown, Wrigley), but most often it is not. This type of sloppy book-keeping is not critical, but it demonstrates a lack of commitment to accuracy and transparency that is disturbing.

Major Errors

Major errors including omitting entire sentence elements. For example, in the case of Edward Hemenway the internal DOJ document lists - "30 days incarceration, $500 restitution," but the actual recommendation is very different – "three months home confinement, followed by a three-year period of probation to include 60 hours of community service, and $500 restitution." These types of errors are substantial and could impact on a person's sentence and therefore, his/her life. What makes this even more confusing is that the GSM for Hemenway lists one set of recommendations in the introductory paragraph and a different set in the conclusion.

Another example is Jonathan Sanders. The GSM (page 1, introduction) says – "… the government requests that this Court sentence Jonathan Sanders to two (2) months home detention, as part of a **3-year term of probation**, 60 hours of community service, and $500 in restitution." On page 17 (conclusion), however, it says – "Balancing these factors, the government recommends that this Court sentence Jonathan Sanders, Sr. to two months of home confinement, **two years of probation**, and $500 in restitution." Apparently, the government internal memo uses the introductory probation recommendation (3 yr.) and not the one listed in the conclusion (2 yr.), but it's difficult to know what the Judge used. Hence, hard to evaluate this one, except to highlight the inconsistencies.

Hemenway and Sanders are not the only instances in which this inconsistency is manifested (cf., Dresch, Gallagher, Palmer, Reimler). How the Judges deal with this sloppiness is unknown, but it does not give anyone confidence in the ability of the DOJ to do their job at a high level.

RESULTS

Overall Comparisons

If you include major and minor errors, only one of the seventy-six cases examined was error- free (Spencer).

Government Sentencing Memorandum

GSMs had thirteen minor and eight major errors. The common

minor error for GSM was the omission of the $10 assessment fee (e.g., Nelson, Markofski, Walden) and the $25 fee (e.g., Courtright, K. Cordon). The fee omission was more troublesome when the fee was $100 (Palmer, Thompson) and when it was applied per count (Fairlamb). Beyond these omissions, the eight major errors in GSM were -

- $500 fine for Jackson Kostolsky was omitted (see page 26).
- $1,000 fine for Karl Dresch was omitted (see page 1).
- 60 hours community service for William Tryon was omitted (see page 21).
- 120 hours of community service for Valerie Ehrke was omitted (see page 4).
- 6 months incarceration for Robert Reeder should have been 2 months (see page 13).
- 3 years supervised release for Cleveland Meredith was omitted (see page 21).
- 1-year supervised release and 60 hours community service for Leonard Ridge was omitted (see page 23).
- 3 months house arrest, 3 years' probation, 60 hours of community service for Edward Hemenway was omitted (see page 1 and page 15).

Disregarding the minor errors, it is impossible to see how fair and accurate sentences can be obtained using this flawed information. The generation of the internal document is not rocket science. It is simply recording and checking. If the DOJ is incapable of such basic skills as accurate recording and checking, how can we rely upon their expertise in more complex tasks?

Judges' Rulings

JR had sixty-four minor errors and ten major errors. The minor errors were the omission of the $10 and $25 assessment fees.

The major errors in JR were the omission of the $100 (Meredith, Palmer, Thompson, Chansley, Hodgkins, Smocks), and $200 (Fairlamb) assessments. In addition -

- $500 restitution was omitted for Michael Rusyn (page 5) and for Sean Cordon (page 5)
- 120 hours of community service for Valerie Ehrke was omitted (see page 4).

Probation Conditions

For some reason, best known to the DOJ, the only conditions of probation that are addressed in the UD is "home detention" or "home confinement." There are nearly a dozen other conditions of probation not addressed. These include substance abuse testing, substance abuse treatment, mental health treatment, mental health medication, social media restrictions, computer search, computer monitoring, re-entry, education, vocational, and employment services. Among the cases examined for this study, one (and usually more) of these elements were used in more than 25% of the total cases and 33% of the cases in which probation was used. In one case 7 of these elements were used and it wasn't unusual for three elements to be used (most often substance abuse and treatment and mental health treatment). Why the DOJ excludes these elements from the internal document is questionable, especially considering what role social media and drug use played in the riot, and also considering how often these elements were used.

General Impressions

Having examined in detail the GSM, here are some overall impressions –

- Information about the defendants is not confined to a single part of the GSM but appears scattered throughout the multi-page documents making it difficult for the Judges to easily get a picture of who the defendant is. Since making a ruling depends somewhat on the character of the defendant, this sloppiness works against a fair and proper process.
- Information about the defendants is often incomplete or missing, even when this applies to such key areas as prior

arrest records, ties to extremist groups, employment, etc. Since making a ruling depends somewhat on the character of the defendant, this missing information works against a fair and proper process.

- Within GSMs there is no consistency in where the final recommendation appears. Sometimes it appears on the first page and sometimes on the last page. Sometimes what appears on the first page is substantially different from what appears on the last page.

CONCLUSION

The DOJ has more than 200 plea agreements and to date has sentenced nearly 100 defendants for their activities in the Jan 6 riot/insurrection. To avoid sentencing disparity and to reach proper decisions, the DOJ created an internal document that purported to accurately describe the previous DOJ sentencing recommendations and the Judge's sentences imposed. By summarizing these results, the DOJ hopes to make the process as fool-proof and valid as possible. Unfortunately, the current research reveals that the DOJ's internal document is deeply flawed, with errors of omission and commission, that could substantially influence the DOJ prosecutors and the Judges to make decisions that are out-of-line with previous decisions, thus opening up the DOJ to appeals based on the inaccurate information used as a basis of the decisions.

PROBLEMS WITH DOJ WEBSITE

In the previous section in this chapter we saw that the data the DOJ and the Judges rely upon is deeply flawed. The memo that I sent to the DOJ was never answered, though a few months after it was sent, there was an improvement in many of the aspects I pointed out. Nonetheless, these problems persist.

In this section I want to provide information about the DOJ website - https://www.justice.gov/usao-dc/capitol-breach-cases. It claims to track everyone "charged in federal court in the District of Columbia" and it provides case number, defendant name, charge(s), case documents, location of arrest, and case status. Under case status they have arrest date, plea agreement date, and sentencing information.

Here are some of the problems

Minor Problems

The DOJ website has the annoying habit of rarely listing the year, which made sense in 2021 when everything was 2021. Now that we're at the end of 2022, the year date would be helpful. 4/28 and 5/7 and 9/14 tell us very little. Next year it will be even more problematic. This problem occurs in about 13% of the cases.

They list most of the people alphabetically, but they use the Jr. and Sr. as if it's a last name in some cases (e.g., Seymour). Not a big deal since it's less than 1%.

Not every J6 case was charged in D.C. so these defendants are missing from the list. This isn't a very long list of defendants (only 2% of total arrested), but if you can't find a name on this list that may be the reason (e.g., Coleman, eBanks, Glosser).

Another reason you might not find a name is those people who died (e.g., Anderson, Barnes), committed suicide (e.g., Aungst, Perna), or otherwise had their case dismissed are also missing. This accounts for more than a dozen people. In some cases they were charged, guilty, and the DOJ put them into a diversion program (e.g., Amos, Doll, Grames). These are all people who met the criteria for listing on the website, but who've been removed. No reason is given.

More Serious Problems

The list of case documents appears to be haphazard and many

that are expected are not present. For example, plea agreements were obtained from dozens of defendants, but these documents did not appear as of Dec 1, 2022. Here are the names of some of the defendants and the date of the plea agreements.

- Bochene – 7/1/2021
- Council – 8/10/2022
- Stallings – 8/24/2022
- P. Young – 11/2/2022

In addition to these omissions, there are times when the case status does not even list the plea agreement date, though it does list the status conference date (e.g., Fitzgerald)

Probably the most important error is that the list of charge(s) on the websites column does not correspond to the complaint's list of charges in the actual complaint form, usually with the list including many more charges than are actually listed in the complaint. Sometimes the list of charges includes felonies that the defendant is not being charged with. FWIW – I did write to the DOJ about this problem, but as usual did not get a reply.

In most cases the complaint form is used for comparisons, but sometimes they don't have the complaint link and instead I used the indictment (e.g., Head).

Here are just some of the examples of discrepancies between what the DOJ lists as charges and what is actually in the complaint. In the first few cases the charges list makes the defendant look worse.

- Fracker lists 5 charges though the complaint has only 2. The list includes felony Obstruction which isn't in the complaint. The charges list not only exaggerates the number of crimes, but also the severity.
- Lyon has 6 charges but the complaint only has 2 (Violent entry and Entering). The list adds felony Obstruction as well as Theft and 2 Disorderly charges. As in the case of Fracker, the charges list exaggerates

the number and severity of crimes.

- Meredith has 4 charges in the list but only 3 in the complaint, The charges add "Possession of Large Capacity Ammunition Feeding Devices."
- Leffingwell has 4 charges but complaint has only 3. DOJ adds "Act of Physical Violence in Capitol Building" to the charges.

Occasionally the charges list makes the defendant look better –

- Languerand lists 4 charges but the complaint has 5. The list is missing theft (18 USC 641).
- Cortez has the same number of charges in the list and the complaint but missing from the list are Assault and Civil Disorder.

Often, it's a mixed bag. The DOJ has more charges listed, thus making the defendant look worse, but then they fail to list a more serious charge.

- Fairlamb has 10 charges listed under charges but only 5 in his complaint. Despite the 10 charges, the list doesn't include Violent Entry (40 USC 5104) or Carrying a Dangerous Weapon (18 USC 1752). Thus, the charges list exaggerates the number of crimes while also not including some more serious crimes.
- Hodgkins lists 5 charges but the complaint only has 3. Missing from the list is Violent Entry.

Almost always the number of charges in the charges list exceeds the complaint number, but not always. For example, C. Meggs had 4 charges in the list but the complaint has 5 charges. Added to the complaint is "Aiding and Abetting" (18 USC 2)

These problems combined occurred in about 40% of the cases listed, Generally speaking, charges in the list exceeded the complaint by about 30%.

All things considered there is no rhyme nor reason in the

mis-matches between what the DOJ claims are charges and what the complaint actually lists as charges. I believe the charges listed in the complaint are more likely to be valid since they appear in a formal document. The list of charges comes from "who knows where?"

Wtf Problems

Perhaps the most serious problem is the occasional failure to list all the sentencing elements in the case status column. For example, in the case of Santillian, the DOJ says – "Sentenced 9/23/22 to 45 days of incarceration, 36 months of probation, and $500 restitution." That's true, but it fails to list Judge Pan's order – "You must complete 60 hours of community service within 24 months." The DOJ does list community service in 160+ cases when it occurred, so the omission here is simply an error, not an example of DOJ choosing to ignore sentencing elements (as they do, for example with house detention).

It's not the only time the DOJ makes this same error (e.g., Jessica Bustle got 40 hours, Robert Chapman got 60, Valerie Ehrke got 120, etc. – none of them are in the DOJ case status column). The errors go both ways. Not only does the DOJ omit community service when it occurs, the DOJ puts it in where it doesn't belong. James Allen Mels is listed as getting 60 hours community service but it's not in the Judge's order. The Munn sisters didn't get the 60 hours the DOJ lists for them as do several others.

Errors like these were not confined to community service. Here are examples of the errors among the 91 fines and the 85 home detention orders –

- DOJ lists Bromley as having a $4,000 fine. In fact, Bromley got $2,000 restitution and a $2,000 fine (as well as a $25 assessment not mentioned on the website).
- DOJ lists Pert with no fine but Judge Friedman's order has $500 fine.

- DOJ lists Zlab with a $500 fine but Judge Walton's order is $5,000.
- DOJ says W. J. Sywak gets no home detention but Judge Contreras order says 60 days.
- DOJ says Ticas gets no home detention but Judge Bates' order says 90 days.

These errors of omission and commission when listing sentencing elements happen in about 6% of the cases listed on the website. In my previous research using the internal DOJ sentencing documents (which are used by prosecutors and judges to set sentences), similar errors were found in over 10% of the 82 cases reviewed then.

Summary

It's pretty clear that the DOJ official website for tracking J6 defendants has lots of errors and the errors are in many categories, including errors of omission and commission as well as plain-and-simple mistakes. These errors can be ascribed to a number of issues starting with the fact that the DOJ fails to explain what the website is, where the data comes from, and how it's updated. This explains some of the errors of omission. The mismatches cannot be explained; nor can the mistakes made with the sentencing elements. I suspect it is just one more example of what a poor job the DOJ is doing.

AFTERMATH

I've been focused on how poorly the DOJ has been doing its job prosecuting the Jan 6 rioters and how lenient the Judges have been. If the Justice system is failing us, reports show that Jan 6 rioters are paying a price at home. Here's a transcript from an interview with one of the rioters (Robert Reeder) -

"This whole ordeal has cost me more than you can imagine. When we started out, you said I can imagine how you feel or what — I've lost my job. I've lost the ability to coach, and Scouts, which was really meaningful to me. I don't even want to go back to my church, which is one of the largest in Maryland. I used to have my son all the time. But my son's name is Robert Reeder. So my son, who had nothing to do with this, is known to feel the effects. And he's now staying with his mother. [SNIFFLES] I don't see it much anymore because she doesn't and he doesn't want to — because of this disgrace. And it's going to follow him around too because of his name. My neighbors won't even talk to me anymore. And we had great relationships. But they all talk and found out. And I'll be walking out to my car, and see them, and I'll say hi, and they won't even say hi back. And that hurts. It's changed the way that I live my life. One of my cures is not to watch the news. I mean, I don't even know what the weather's going to be."

JOB PROBLEMS

So, while the DOJ gives unprecedented leniency to the Jan 6 defendants, the greater community is not so kind. Over 100 people lost their jobs, either by being fired or resigning. Some of these people (e.g., Therese Duke, Jennifer Gugger, Matthew Clark, Caitlin and Alexander Everett) were not arrested but were fired or resigned after it was discovered that they attended the event. The figure below shows numbers by job category.

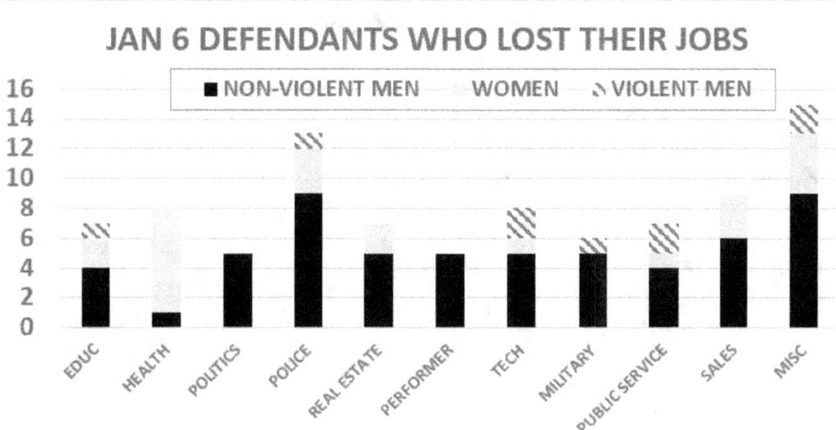

Looking at the data on people being fired, resigning, or suspended, they were more than 10% of those arrested. Bear in mind that many of the people arrested were retired (e.g., W. Merry) unemployed (e.g., C. Bingert, J. Khater, C. Meredith, G. Miller), homeless (e.g., E. Jackson, E. Aesfyza), disabled (T. Caldwell), students (e.g., E. Irizarry, R. Zink, G. Courtright) or a "homemaker" (e.g., J. Bustle). Taking into account these people who were not in the labor pool, the percent of people who suffered job loss for their actions amounts to closer to 20% of those apprehended.

Certain jobs were more "at risk" for consequences. These were law enforcement, education, and sales positions. Laborers who constituted a sizeable portion of the non-violent male offenders were less likely to suffer consequences. On a percentage basis, people in the health industry (e.g., nurses, therapists), education, and law enforcement, were more at risk for consequences than people in other sectors.

Women were more likely to suffer as a result – 18%. For violent men it was only 3% and for non-violent men it was 14%. One reason for this discrepancy is that women were more likely to come from high-risk occupations while violent men were not.

OTHER PROBLEMS

In addition to job loss, some people experienced other types of problems –

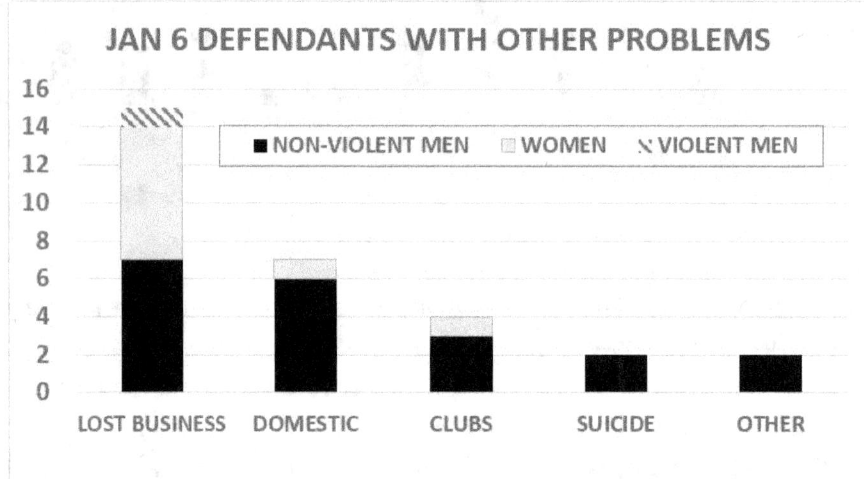

Most of the domestic problems involved divorce, but some involved custody battles, children moving out, and general alienation. Women lost proportionately more business than men.

TEARS AND BEGGING

More than a dozen rioters were reported to cry, sob, beg, and/or tear-up following their arrest. They were mostly men but included some women. Almost all had been charged with a felony, most commonly Obstruction, but also Assault, Assault with a Deadly Weapon, Civil Disorder, and Conspiracy. On average they faced 10+ years maximum jail time. Almost all were White. Women averaged 42 years' old (31 to 55), as did men (18-68).

The median size city was 44,259 people which was nearly twice the median size for the other rioters.

Only 7% had a BA or higher degree. None were professionals and only 7% were managers. A high proportion (33%) were small business owners. The average rioter contained more professionals (7%), fewer business owners (16%), and more college graduates (38%).

Though a high percent of rioters were arrested with another family member, among people who broke down, there were few examples of co-defendant relatives.

Compared to the average rioter, rioters who broke down were significantly more inclined to come to D.C. with violent intentions (73% v 61%), less inclined to be looking for meaning (0% v 5%), social reasons (0% v 5%) or oppose the election results (27% v 33%), and more inclined to support Trump (33% v 19%) and look for violence (20% v 15%). A high percent had prior arrest records (67%) including nearly 30% for assault. Almost half had ties to extremist groups, the most common being 3%ers and militia members. None were known to associate with Proud Boys, Second Amendment groups, or White Supremacists.

In summary, comparing rioters who "broke down" with those who didn't, they were similar in average age, age range, race, and the presence of known mental health problems, with slightly more women among those who broke down. What dramatically distinguished the rioters who broke down in <u>demographics</u> were the larger town size, higher percent of people charged with felonies, more small business owners, and fewer college graduates.

What distinguished the rioters who broke down from the other rioters in <u>pre-riot behavior</u> was the inclination of those who broke down to be more focused on Trump and violence and less concerned with the election, finding meaning, or using the trip for social reasons. Those who later broke down were less likely to be associated with extremist groups and less likely to come with a relative.

In actual <u>riot and post-riot behavior</u>, those who broke down were almost twice as inclined to commit a violent act but nearly equally inclined to plead (53% v 48%).

Bear in mind, the relatively small number of rioters who "broke down" makes it difficult to generalize from this data, especially when the differences are small. However, large differences are worthy of note and bear examining as more data comes in.

So, what does this all mean, apart from the data itself? I look at this as a double avoidance conflict (DAC). Rioters who have a lot to lose don't want to lose what they have, and they also want to avoid the punishment that's coming. DACs often produce anxiety, for obvious reasons, and often more anxiety than other conflict situations.

The rioters who broke down had more to lose than the average rioter, as shown by the abnormally high percent of business owners. They also faced much higher punishment than the average rioter due to their higher violent crimes. With more to lose and facing greater punishment, anxiety would be significantly higher.

The only way to reduce anxiety in this case is to plead, and hope that the ruling will be favorable, or at least, not as punitive as expected. In any event, pleading will stop the "anticipatory" anxiety. Mediating factors such as the higher percent of women and the fewer ties to extremist groups means that "standing their ground" wasn't necessary. Extremists who expect the end of the world will keep believing the world will end even when it doesn't, because their need to cling to the cult is so strong it mediates more logical decision making. But here the rioters don't have that need: even the extremist groups they had ties to were not the "hard-core" groups.

Facing DACs and increasing anxiety, these rioters broke down. For rioters with less to lose, or rioters facing less punishment, the anxiety would be substantially less and the likelihood of breaking down much less.

SUMMARY

I've placed this chapter next to last because many of you may be getting depressed from learning what a poor job the DOJ is doing. Putting that aside, the people who broke down and the people who lost their jobs or businesses, or marriages show that other factors beyond the DOJ are at work.

In total, 15% of the people arrested experienced some type of major problem including job loss, divorce, child custody, and suicide. Bear in mind these are only the people we know about. There may be far more. Also bear in mind that a significant percent of the population was unemployed, retired, homeless, or disabled – meaning, the 15% of the total 900+ defendants is, in terms of the job environment, closer to 25%. I hope you take some solace from the fact that everyday Americans are not as lenient as the DOJ.

SUMMARY AND CONCLUSION

"…the limited political democracy that still exists is hanging by a delicate thread." **Noam Chomsky, Jan 6, 2022.**

The purpose of this investigation was to determine whether sentencing for the Jan 6 defendants was more or less restrictive than the types of punishments given out for other kinds of defendants. This task was not a simple one, made complex because there are a half dozen different charges, punishment for each charge can included up to five different elements, little data is available for every aspect that requires investigation, the characteristics of the defendants range widely apart from the over-representation of White people, the lists of Judges and DOJ prosecutors is long, especially the prosecutors, and in some cases, the number of defendants for a particular study is small. Despite these difficulties, data was collected, analyzed, and in many cases definitive results were obtained.

Yes.

The answer to the question of whether or not Jan 6 defendants are getting a light ride is "Yes." "Definitely Yes." Compared to the normal people convicted in federal court of similar offenses, Jan 6 defendants generally get treated better in almost every respect. Where they get equal or worse treatment, there is usually an explanation. For example, Jan 6 defendants took longer to move from arrest to sentencing but considering the Jan 6 arrests presented the DOJ with the single largest case in their history, during a Pandemic, the slight delay is understandable. Jan 6 defendants generally got more probation attached to their jail sentences, but their chances of going to jail were less and the time spent in jail was also less, so that seems to compensate for the longer probation time.

To get a handle on comparable arrests and sentencing for people who protested, research was done on the BLM protesters, more than 90% of whom engaged in peaceful protests. The thought was that if the Jan 6 defendants are being treated more leniently, perhaps it's the case that people convicted of a crime when protesting are treated more leniently than people otherwise convicted of similar offenses (e.g., obstruction, trespass, disorderly). This research revealed that far from being treated leniently, BLM protesters were treated far more harshly that Jan 6 defendants or the general population. Thus, the results reveal a continuum on almost every measure, from Jan 6 defendants to the general population to the BLM protesters. Seemingly, there is a premium placed on people before the Justice system who are right-wingers, and possibly this premium extends to race, with Jan 6 defendants being 90%, Whites in jail about 60%, and Whites arrested in BLM protests about 25%. The Whiter you are, the less punishment you're likely to get. This is not the first time research revealed this shameful result.

A simple "Yes" to the main question this book addresses isn't sufficient without the obvious follow-up question – "How much?" Looking only at the comparisons with the normal defendants convicted of similar offenses -

- Jan 6 offenders were less likely to be apprehended, despite the largest fugitive hunt in history.
- Upon arrest, Jan 6 defendants were more likely to be released on their own recognizance.
- Jan 6 defendants were more likely to get their "day in court" rather than settle their case through a plea agreement.
- Judges were more than twice as likely to rule in favor of Jan 6 defendants compared to the usual federal

defendant.

- Jan 6 defendants got less jail time compared to people convicted of misdemeanors or disorderly conduct.

By anyone's estimate, the leniency shown Jan 6 defendants is substantial and meaningful.

The next obvious question is "Why?" What accounts for these differences which seem to appear at every stage in the Justice system, from identification to arrest, pre-trial judgment, plea agreements, and sentencing? Surely it cannot be the nature of the crime. The research indicates that this was not a "MAGA tourist event" or a "rally gone badly;" rather, it was a planned event where more than half the people involved either had prior arrest records or came to the event with specific plans to commit violence. Bear in mind, the event was not merely a protest, but it was planned to be a protest that specifically intended to disrupt the elected officials from pursuing their constitutional obligations. If not "treason," the planners are surely guilty of "insurrection" or at least "seditious conspiracy," and the participants, almost all of whom were aware of the purpose of the assault, could similarly be charged, or at the very least, charged with "aiding and abetting" the insurrection. Compared to people arrested for trespassing onto a freeway or into a building to support any cause, the people arrested for Jan 6 should be treated more harshly.

Putting aside the fact that the crime itself is more heinous than most other misdemeanor charges that come before the federal bench, the people so charged are, in general, more likely to have a criminal record and more likely to belong to extremist groups most of whom advocate violence.

Leniency for _this_ crime for _these_ people is unthinkable, yet it is what has happened.

Some people have excused the leniency by saying that it's early in the prosecution and the DOJ has chosen "low hanging fruit" and is using these light sentences to clear the boards so they can concentrate on the more important cases. While it's possible, some of the people chosen are hardly "low hanging fruit", such as the widely publicized QAnon Sharman, the Olympic Gold medal winner, or the 240-pound MMA Fighter. Moreover, light sentences now make it much more difficult to switch mid-stream to harsher sentences. Already, early in the process, defendants are arguing that their sentences are out-of-line with previous lighter sentences, and those sentences to which they refer might still be considered light. Generally speaking, Judges are required "to avoid sentence disparities among defendants with similar records who are guilty of similar conduct." The light sentences given so far make it difficult for Judges to switch to harsher sentences going forward. Therefore, the likelihood that lighter sentences are a strategic ploy used by Prosecutors and Judges is doubtful.

Can the relative leniency shown to Jan 6 rioters be a function of their harmless behavior? Some will (and do) argue that most of the defendants charged so far were not guilty of anything more than being in the wrong place at the wrong time, harmed no one, stole nothing, and destroyed nothing. Hence, light sentences should be given. That argument flies in the face of reality. Among the 300+ people sentenced, more than a dozen were originally charged with felonies including assault, physical violence, weapons possession, interstate threats, conspiracy, property destruction, theft, and obstruction. In their zeal to get plea agreements, almost all these charges disappeared. On average, 3 to 5 charges were reduced by DOJ prosecutors to a single misdemeanor charge (usually "Parading"). Even if there weren't such a heavy presence of felonious behavior, the vast majority of defendants were not passive tourists. They cheered, broke down already shattered windows, threw barricades aside, used social media to boast of the events, yelled profanities at the Police, and otherwise contributed to a situation in which two people died on site, three more died later, and 150 Police and dozens of rioters were injured, many of them hospitalized. Here are just a few examples, based on FBI reports –

36-year-old Andrew Bennett from Maryland, wearing a Proud Boys hat, chanted "break it down," encouraging the crowd to break down the entrance to the Speaker's room. He wasn't charged with "aiding and abetting."

University of Kentucky 23-year-old senior Gracyn Courtright was found walking inside the Capitol with the "Member's Only" sign. She wasn't charged with theft.

23-yead-old student Andrew Ericson livestreamed himself taking a beer from Speaker Pelosi's refrigerator. He wasn't charged with theft.

Aaron Mostofsky, son of a Brooklyn judge, was captured in a photo carrying a Capitol Police shield and wearing an officer's bullet proof vest. He wasn't charged with theft.

34-year-old unemployed Russel Peterson was captured on video smashing a window and yelling "This is our house. Let us in." He wasn't charged with "aiding and abetting."

36-year-old Devlyn Thompson from Columbus Ohio posed with a coat rack. When questioned by Police he dropped the coat rack and fled. He wasn't charged with theft.

These are only a few examples.

Carissa Byrne Hessick, a professor at the University of North Carolina School of Law and an expert on plea bargaining, noted in a BuzzFeed interview - "It strikes me that the people who entered the Capitol did something a lot more than that. They didn't just go somewhere they weren't supposed to be, but they went there for a particular reason. And it was a pretty bad one: They wanted to stop votes from being counted and they wanted to stop the election from being certified. I hope people will see how much efficiency is weighing into the calculus here and ask why we're running our justice system this way."

No, there is no overwhelmingly good conduct that merits such leniency. The appearance of good behavior is a result of the DOJ dropping felony charges for almost every one of the defendants originally charged with a felony.

Can the leniency be explained by the right-wing Judges appointed by Donald Trump ruling in favor of the people who defended the man who gave them their jobs? It's tempting, but it doesn't fit with the facts. True, Trump-appointed Judges have been the most lenient of any other group of Judges, but leniency has been a feature of Biden (Cobb, Pan) and Obama appointees (Boasberg, Howell, Moss, Jackson) as well as Reagan (Hogan) and Bush (Bates) appointees. Nor can leniency be ascribed to the women Judges, though there is a suggestion that without Judge Chutkan, the rest of the non-White Judges tend to be more lenient. Overall, however, leniency among judges doesn't seem to have any reliable indicator. It looks pervasive, with only a few exceptions – Obama-appointed 59-year-old Chutkan and Reagan-appointed 68-year-old Lamberth. In any event, the difference made by the Judges (lowering the DOJ recommendations by an average of a few weeks) are insubstantial against the way the DOJ prosecutors reduced the charges from an average of 4+ to a single charge, eliminated most felonies, and made recommendations that reduced the average jail time substantially.

So, what about these DOJ prosecutors? The leniency shown to the Jan 6 defendants appears to come from their actions at several levels. Unfortunately, there are dozens of DOJ prosecutors, and very few managed more than a few cases. As a result, looking at the characteristics of the prosecutors won't produce much usable information. There is a hint that most Prosecutors are getting their recommendations cast aside and Judges are doing their own thing, usually handing down a ruling that was less harsh than the one the prosecutors recommended. More data would be helpful. It's hard to fathom how Judges would be even more lenient given the leniency already shown by the prosecutors in reducing charges from 4+ to 1, removing dozens of felony charges, and using penalties that were already seriously downsized from what could be used. These facts require we go elsewhere for an explanation.

Does the problem come from the top? When seeking appointment, Attorney General Garland spoke about Jan 6 in profoundly serious tones, yet the Wall Street Journal in October 2021 reported that Garland told DOJ officials that "he is concerned that jailing rioters who weren't hard-core extremists for extensive periods could further radicalize them." Before Congress, Garland later claimed his comments were taken out of context, but failed to indicate the context they should be taken in. He continues to insist that the prosecutors are allowed to pursue the defendants without interference, but he also refuses to acknowledge that their responses have not reflected the seriousness of the situation he claims to recognize. Either Garland is a hypocrite or an incompetent administrator. The idea of allowing your subordinates freedom is an excellent one if they achieve desirable results. If their performance falters, an effective administrator must stop watching and jump in. If Jan 6 was a serious assault on democracy, as Garland claims it was, and if his Department isn't bringing home the bacon, it's time for Garland to act. Instead, Garland worries that harsh treatment may radicalize the people who are not "hard-core." Well and good, but as this research reveals, at least half of the defendants so far sentenced have prior arrest histories, ties to extremist groups, and came to D.C. prepared to use violence. If these facts don't define "hard-core", what definition does Garland have in mind?

Even more disturbing, on the one-year anniversary of January 6, Garland spoke at length and among other things he said - "...these acts and threats of violence are not associated with any one set of partisan or ideological views." Given the research to date, Garland's remarks fly in the face of the facts. January 6 was a direct expression of partisan and ideological views that have been stoked for four years by the former President and his right-wing sycophants. If Garland is unaware of this, he's even more incompetent than any of his critics ever imagined. One columnist wrote – "...his insistence that threats against local officials are not limited to any particular political persuasion is an insult to our collective intelligence."

Clearly the expressed fears of AG Garland to not go hard on the Jan 6 defendants is at play in understanding what happened. Combined with his apparent inability to examine and manage what is occurring, his "go soft" approach provides some explanation for what is happening. Yet by itself, it hardly is a sufficient cause, even if a necessary one.

Having exhausted the alternative explanations, one alarming and disturbing explanation remains – few people in the Justice system take the events of January 6 seriously. Despite the comments of many of the prosecutors and Judges, their behavior suggests that they view the bulk of the January 6 defendants as patriotic Americans who, however misguided, were exercising their First Amendment rights and, unintentionally, got pulled into a riot. They ignore the prior arrest histories, the ties to extremist groups, the violent intentions, and the fact that so many defendants didn't even bother to vote in 2020. They see the White faces and the middle-aged bodies, and almost all of the DOJ employees are uniformly unable to pull the trigger.

Is the problem that they don't have this information to guide their decisions, or have they done such a poor job in preparing for the cases that good scholarship has been ignored? Let's see. Every one of the multiple page documents called "Government's Sentencing Memorandum" contains a section called "The History and Character of the Offender" or some equivalent. A lot of the information about the defendants is included here, but the truth is that there is little consistency between reports, and relevant information is likely to pop up anywhere. In documents that can be 30 pages or longer, trying to get a sense of whom a Judge is dealing with can be difficult. Comparing my database against the information contained in that section (and elsewhere) provides a good idea of the extent to which the DOJ prosecutors marshalled the available evidence in order to make an appropriate recommendation, bearing in mind the prosecutor's guidelines discussed earlier which require them to ferret out the most serious offense.

Generally speaking, the DOJ Sentencing Memorandum has

a random selection of facts about the defendants, sometimes mentioning marital status, children, financial ability, and education. They do a better job discussing prior arrest records and occupation, though even here the work is hardly exemplary and there are gaps where there shouldn't be (recall the case of Dana Winn). They may comment that someone has "stable employment" without mentioning the kind of job or the income. They don't do a particularly good job in identifying people with extremist ties, and they usually focus on post-riot social media comments rather than pre-riot comments. If I were grading the prosecutors, I'd give them, collectively, a "C-", noting that a few submissions are very good, and some are remarkably poor. This problem undoubtedly contributes to the leniency being shown to the defendants since truly relevant facts are either ignored or difficult to find. Without this information, Judges may be inclined to think that they are dealing with the person next door, rather than the organized people intent on violence who already had committed various crimes, and many of whom had extremist ties.

If AG Garland's preference to "go soft" on the defendants and his inability to manage what's happening are necessary though not sufficient causes of the leniency, and if the haphazard DOJ recommendations denying Judges complete information about the defendants is another contributing factor, are these two factors sufficient to account for the leniency shown to people who literally tried to disrupt the government? Probably not. That leaves a third element, hinted at earlier. The people in charge of seeking justice for the January 6 defendants are simply looking at this case as something akin to peaceful protests by patriots who were misguided by a toxic media and misled by a narcissistic President. Repeatedly, from the defendants, the prosecutors, and the Judges, the argument is made that the defendants were innocent pawns, lured into misbehaving, and now that they see the errors of their ways, everything will be OK. Prosecutors and Judges hunt for any inclinations from the defendants that they're "sorry" or "repentant" or "ashamed". Every tear and every sorrowful nod secure another month taken from a sentence or another $100 reduced from a fine. The prosecutors and the Judges are existing in a fantasy world of their own making, christened by the AG, and reinforced by the Senators and Representatives who spend their time pursuing the ex-President, while ignoring the actions of the boots on the ground. Of course, the President and his minions need to be held accountable for their actions, but if the people who invaded the Capitol, attacked and harmed the Police, destroyed property and stole what they could carry, are not punished appropriately, what is to stop a future and more violent event?

We stand at a critical place in our Nation's history. Not since the Civil War has the very nature of our Democracy been challenged. All of us need to be involved in helping the Nation heal and in avoiding future, even worse events. Part of the healing involves people taking responsibility for what they did and for the Government to hold them accountable. Hence this book and the data which shows that the Department of Justice is failing in its mission. Yet the re-invigoration of the DOJ is not sufficient without dealing with the issues that prompted the insurrection and the sequalae – economic inequality and racial prejudices are probably the two most relevant issues underlying what happened on Jan 6.

Professor Barbara Walter has an interesting perspective. Having studied civil wars across the world she concluded there are "...really only two factors, best predicted where civil war was likely to break out. The first was what we called anocracy, that's a fancy term for partial democracy, and the second factor was whether a country's population began to break down into racial, ethnic or religious political parties." She concluded - "So the two big factors that we know are warning signs for civil wars in countries outside the United States we're now seeing here."

Macro issues need to be dealt with, but these are larger issues and will take time to remedy: for here and now, the performance of the DOJ should be changed. Here are some recommendations –

-        The formula for determining the costs of the insurrection needs to be completely overhauled and future fines need to reflect the real costs.

-        Special terms of probation need to address computer monitoring and meeting with extremist groups where appropriate (which applied in more than half the cases).

-        Problems of accuracy throughout the DOJ paperwork need to be remedied, from internal memos to sentencing recommendations

-    The Government Sentencing Memorandums need to be dramatically revised. They need to be standardized, errors of omission need to be eliminated, and the section on the Nature and Characteristics of the Defendant needs to be improved and expanded.

-        The DOJ website needs to be improved. Data is incomplete and often weeks behind. Often there are errors. Summaries of what has happened need to be included.

-        Reports to the public should be issued every month. These reports should include relevant data on the defendants as well as summaries.

Unless dramatic changes are made within the DOJ, the Nation is doomed for more and possibly worse events.

ABOUT THE AUTHOR

Dr. James Gardner is an internationally acclaimed academic, researcher, and clinician with more than two dozen books and over 100 articles in major international journals. Following his doctorate at Ohio State University, he was Director of Clinical and Community Psychology at the University of Queensland (Australia) and Professor and Head of Applied Psychology at the University of the Witwatersrand (South Africa).

In addition to his academic credits, he founded a software development company and an internet marketing company and worked as a Management Consultant to Fortune 500 companies. In addition, he was elected to the Lake Forest (CA) City Council and served as Mayor. Among his many awards he was elected to the Honor Society in Psychology, "Outstanding Man of the Year" by Columbus (Ohio) Jaycees, Volunteer of the Year by the Queensland Mental Health Society and Orange County Breast Cancer Survivors, and was recognized by the Orange County Board of Supervisors for his work with animal welfare. On the next page are some books that may interest you. They are all available on Amazon in eBook and paperback.

INSURRECTION: THE RIOT

Everything you wanted to know about the Capitol riot including all the antecedents, minute-by-minute details, charges, arrests, groups involved, individuals, weapons used, motivation of those people arrested, aftermath, job problems, sentencing, etc. Includes modal profiles of violent offenders, female offenders, and the notorious non-violent offenders as well as outliers in each category. Data about

military involvement, active and former law enforcement, the role of extremist groups. how rioters differ from each other and from the average U.S. citizens, etc.

TRUMP NATIONS

Who are the 70 million plus people who voted for Donald Trump and how do they differ from the rest of America? This book examines 50 different variables (e.g., IQ, life expectancy, income, health, religion, race, alcoholism, hate groups, gun ownership, etc.) in 7 major areas (Intelligence, Health, Family Life, Religiosity, Economics, Personality, Voter Behavior) to discover how Trump voters differ from Biden voters how they differ among each other. You'll discover there isn't a single Trump Nation but different and distinct groups that make up the Trump Nations. You'll also learn where they are and more importantly you'll discover the underlying motivations that propel them and help explain how we got here and where we need to go.

www.ingramcontent.com/pod-product-compliance
Lightning Source LLC
Chambersburg PA
CBHW070128260726
48658CB00001B/317